PUBLISHER'S NOTE

Many people will probably fail to recognize the Villa d'Este they toured and admired, guidebook duly in hand, in the Villa d'Este they will encounter thanks to Leonardo dal Maso. The words of the author are particularly evocative as we are led back into the past and look behind the façade of the villa as it appears today, discovering the reality of the remarkable and erudite « architectural garden » designed and brought to life four hundred years ago. Leonardo Dal Maso is certainly not new to such original cultural undertakings, the final result of which is essentially a recovery of a long buried, long forgotten heritage. Before the VILLA D'ESTE, he accomplished this noteworthy deed in other books written for Bonechi: « Rome of the Caesars, » « Rome of the Popes, » and « Archaeological Latium, » this latter in collaboration with Roberto Vighi. In short Dal Maso's signature is a hallmark of originality and scholarly rigor, perfectly blended in easily read texts.

Now we are ready to enter the Villa d'Este. It was built for a great and enlightened Renaissance cardinal: Ippolito d'Este. Ippolito was the son of Alfonso, third duke of Ferrara and his notorious wife, Lucrezia Borgia. The villa was designed by Pirro Ligorio, the renowned and celebrated Neapolitan archtitect who created a composition of such scenic impact for his patron Ippolito that it would be copied over and over again throughout Europe.

Dal Maso is somehow able to make the reader relive all the stages in the creation of the villa, such as the incredible feat of levelling the mountain of Tivoli, the building of the aqueducts, and the designing of the staircases and ramps. Each stage is brought to life with Dal Maso's special outlook: he does not limit himself to just seeing, he also wants to know, and when he knows, he then wants to fully understand. To achieve these goals, he goes further than collecting and analyzing facts and data, studying documents and prints of the day, carefully taking measurements of walls and paths, counting out the scudi that the generous Cardinal handed out: he tries to become part of those times and those personages—it is almost as if he wants to think with their heads and see through their eyes. And the fountains are not only remarkable decorative elements but the whole, marbles and plants, walks and pauses, water and land, is firmly interwoven into a single symbolic message, like a mythical fairytale whose language is unfortunately lost to us.

EDOARDO BONECHI

3

Panoramic view of the city of Tivoli from the terrace of the villa with the fountain made out of an antique tripod from Hadrian's Villa.

LEONARDO B. DAL MASO

THE VILLA
OF IPPOLITO II D'ESTE
AT TIVOLI

BONECHI EDIZIONI «IL TURISMO» - FIRENZE

We would like to thank Cinzia Dal Maso for her kind help in researching the sections on mythology.

Reproductions: La Fotolitografia, Florence

ISBN 88-7204-144-9

THE TYPOLOGICAL DEVELOPMENT
OF THE ITALIAN VILLA
FROM ITS ORIGINS TO THE 16TH CENTURY

The villas built in Italy over the centuries have together constituted a typological phenomenon systematically bound to the structure of the garden. Such phenomenon was more widespread and entailed more diversification than anywhere else. The evolution of the villas, determined by particular economic, social, and cultural conditions, went hand in hand with the country's historical and political development and was at times clearly the result of the close cooperation that grew up between the artist and his patron (the latter often being spurred on by the same desire to attain prestige that had led the aristocratic families to build themselves luxurious dwellings).

The prime example came from the Romans for whom the villa had represented a way to arrive at a more direct contact with nature based upon agriculture and their love for country living. Moreover, as Cicero put it, a restful stay in the villa meant that the city dweller could achieve intellectual self-fulfillment sublimating his own individuality far from the hectic city life. In the city, he noted, even the homes of the very wealthy were modest since, on account of the overcrowded urbanistic structure, i.e. heavily built up neighborhoods and narrow roadways, it was impossible for the city to spread out. On the other hand, the villa gave the well-to-do Romans the opportunity to show off their wealth, not only by the size and number of buildings the villa was composed of, but also by the profusion of works of art with which it was embellished.

As was true of every work of architecture, the villa played an important part in the history of Roman building: a whole branch of literature ranging from Cato to Varro bears witness to the Romans' agricultural heritage, while Vitruvius set forth practical norms for the rational spatial layout of buildings. Yet we cannot speak of a real typology of the

villa, which continued to follow the general development of civil architecture and which is thus often compared to the development of the domus.

*The utilitarian aspect of the Roman villa is shown time and time again by its division into agricultural and residential sections. This division first appears in the 3rd century B.C. in keeping with changes in Roman economic and social life. Thus, the villa was composed of two clearly distinctive buildings: the « rustic » villa, constructed like rural buildings, and the « urban » villa. The rustic villa was built to house the farmhands and their foreman (*vilicus*) and included storerooms, stalls, granaries. Since aesthetic considerations played no part, it was strictly a work of construction engineering. On the other hand, the urban villas, generally set into a spacious sea or landscape, was designed for the owner of the whole complex and was thus a reflection of his personal taste and financial possibilities. Nevertheless, it is also true that not all the villas displayed such a distinction, as several consisted of a single building set into landscaped and wooded areas.*

The patrician villa, more complex since it consisted of several constructions, had geometric gardens symmetrically laid out so that, together with the buildings, the garden was an element added to the surrounding landscape.

*The art of garden architecture (*ars topiaria*) was born towards the end of the Republican period, based upon the examples of Lucullus in his villa at the Pincio and Sallust in the gardens between the Quirinal and the Porta Collina. Plinius attributes the origin of the art of garden architecture to C. Mazius Calvena, who was a friend of the Emperor Augustus.*

The Roman garden in its simplicity pivoted around a central clearing with a decorative fountain in the center. Radiating from this space were the main pathways, some of which were meant for walks (ambulationes), while other broader paths were for drives in litters (gestationes). Sometimes the pathways were shaded by pergolas sustained by marble columns or caryatids. They were bounded by flowerbeds with herbs and flowers and were interspersed with tiny trees pruned into all sorts of shapes. Spaced between the trees were box hedges, also fashioned in various shapes. The hedges were low enough to allow a view of the landscape and statuary, benches, and vases set here and there among the pathways. Thus, the duties of the architectural gardener (topiarius) which entailed a host of activities not specifically related to gardens, actually involved both architecture and sculpture. Frequently, these garden architects revealed great skill in creating obelisks, pyramids, statues, and animals out of plants. Their garden landscapes were so highly appreciated that they would often be reproduced in the murals frescoed in the villas along with country scenes of animals, flowers, and trees.

By the same token, the villa itself would later constitute one of the basic elements of Roman landscape painting, often closely tied in with motifs of the sea animal world, by this time widely used in all Roman decorative art.

Hand in hand with their passion for the artistic layout of plants in gardens, the Romans also delighted in making water an integral part of the vegetable and architectural elements. Besides natural waterways, the villas contained pools stocked with fish, tiny canals, and artificial waterfalls with reflecting pools.

In the early stages, the fountains were in the form of cascades flowing down the walls of natural grottos. Later, they were set into artificial grottos or nymphaeums replete with ceilings, niches, and apses decorated with seashells, mother-of-pearl, and statuary. The fountains themselves were made up either of statues, singly or in groups, portraying figures from the sea or Dionysian worlds, or else they were in the form of craters, at times with jets that emitted odd-sounding noises. In addition, water was used to power hydraulic organs, one of the best-known being the « Hydraulus » created by Ctesibius, the Alexandrian mathematician. Nero is known to have been exceedingly fond of such organs.

By the end of Rome's Imperial Age, the custom of constructing villas had fallen into disuse and throughout the High Middle Ages we find only castles. Within the castle walls there were gardens, though usually not exceedingly large, with lawns, flowerbeds, ornamental fountains, carved benches and fruit trees, as the miniatures in the codices prove. The cloisters of the monasteries and convents were wholly or partially landscaped and within their walls grew medical herbs, vegetables, fruit trees, and flowers. There were even fountains, sometimes set in little squares off to one side of the porticoed courtyards.

Around the year 1000, attempts at suburban and rural decentralizing cropped up here and there, on the heels of the cultural and social reawakening then in act. Nevertheless, it was not until the 13th century that we find a return to the custom of building country homes. This was brought about by various factors, such as the decline of feudalism, the renewal of agriculture on a more organized basis, and the transformation of the castles into more comfortable dwellings.

The gradual return to a less dangerous life style, which spanned the period from the end of the 13th to the beginning of the 14th centuries, led to a new flourishing of the villas, as we learn from the chronicles of the time. For instance, the chronicler Giovanni Villani reports that the noble and well-to-do citizens of Florence « ... spent four months a year in the country, together with their families. » In the words of an anonymous Ticenese author (1320), there were villas in Pavia, « .... for the recreation of the citizens. » Boccaccio in the Decameron gives an exemplary description of what a 14th century villa was like: a magnificent palace with numerous luxuriously furnished rooms built around a central courtyard and enhanced by a splendid setting. Boccaccio added the element that a stay in a villa also entailed intellectual delights.

Descriptions of gardens have also come down to us in the words of the chroniclers and writers of the times. Most commonly cited are the preface to the third day in the Decameron and the first four chapters of the eighth book of « Agriculture » by Pietro de' Crescenzi. Naturally, these gardens were composed of only elementary geometric patterns, and had no particularly outstanding artistic motifs.

From the 14th century stirrings to the dawn of the 15th century, we can define the basis of the Renaissance villa which was then evolving into regional variants. All the variants however had a common bond in the Humanistic spirit which from the Medici court was spreading throughout Italy, indeed throughout the whole of Europe. People in the regions of Liguria, Lombardy, and Venice, favored by political and economic incentives, either began to adapt pre-existing buildings into dwellings in keeping with the new Renaissance ideals or else enthusiastically threw themselves into the job of creating new villas from scratch. Likewise, the courts of Rome and Naples, also permeated with Humanism and anxious to partake of the new cultural atmosphere, undertook a whole series of architectural initiatives, the villa being one of the most important of these.

Structurally speaking, the early Quattrocento villas were rather vast buildings, at times two storied, with a single tower or a pair of towers flanking the central section. On the ground floor was a loggia which led up to the entrance to the main hall.

Michelozzo is credited with being the first architect to have turned castles and fortresses into country homes, intentionally refining the stolid campactness of medieval architecture. Yet at times it

Bagnaia, Villa Lante: frescoes in the loggia of the Palazzina Gambara. Above: Villa d'Este in Tivoli, from the engraving by Dupérac which shows the original design, below: the Villa Lante with its garden and park (1587-1588).

was technically impossible to put such innovations into practice and so he turned his attention to the surrounding space. Here he performed his transformations or created new settings so that the garden would become a more attractive place. In the villas of Trebbio (1427), Cafaggiolo (1451), and Careggi (1457) Michelozzo forged a synthesis between the old and the new.

Even though theoretical studies on the Roman villa had been one of the favorite subjects taken up by Renaissance architects, at first they failed to make actual imitations, mainly since they had no models to copy. In fact, their passion for archaeological excavations went no further than digging up works of art and never to the point of unearthing entire building complexes. Moreover, the new architecture, restricted to a well-defined social group, was confined to a definite type of edifice. The real nature of the Renaissance villa only emerged in the second half of the 15th century when the owner of the villa, now that the new philosophical and literary concepts had come to be accepted, saw his Humanistic ideals enacted in his country home (otia in « locus amoenus »).

These concepts were developed by the Humanist architect Leon Battista Alberti in his « De Re Aedificatoria. » Through the study of Latin texts, Alberti sought first of all to pick out the social reasons that led to the birth and development of the Roman villa, though he never neglected at the same time to study both their perspective and proportions (and, in fact, he was one of the first to master these arts). Simultaneously he took up a study of the social structure of his times whereby he attributed a specific building to each of the social classes; thus, the structure and function of the nobleman's villa derive from the city building, whereas the rural building is characteristic of the bourgeoisie.

Another who devoted himself to studies on the villa, albeit from a different outlook, was Francesco di Giorgio Martini. Although he closely followed the precepts of Vitruvius and Alberti, his studies were confined to the practical problems involved in construction and the relationship between garden and villa.

A return to the Roman models as an attempt to achieve a new, well-defined type of villa, came about towards the end of the 15th century when the medieval tradition had been wholly abandoned. These architectural concepts were used as a model by Giuliano da Sangallo in the villa he designed at Poggio a Caiano (near Florence) for Lorenzo de' Medici. The villa is inspired by Roman art in the simplicity of the layout and the technique used in blending the elements harmoniously conceived in accordance with the canons set forth by Alberti. Here the Humanistic view of country life held by a political man involved in both agriculture and his favorite intellectual pursuits is expressed in the frieze over the trabeation of the entrance.

Theories and principles were formulated for gardens as well. The garden was conceived as the link between the building and the countryside. Specific treatises, such as Francesco Colonna's « Hypnerotomachia Poliphili » were also used as reference points. There is a revival of elements belonging to Roman gardens, such as the geometric patterns of the flowerbeds, plants shaped by pruning, column pergolas, benches, grottos, vases, and fountains. Once again antique and contemporary statues peopled the pathways, while flowers, no longer the dominant element, were relegated to secret gardens in special zones. Grass labyrinths, exotic plants, islands dotting ponds, and secret gardens are only a few on the novelties of the 15th century garden. In addition, innovations of a more practical nature, such as the use of uneven surfaces by means of terracing and wide-tread staircases (e.g. Villa Medici in Fiesole near Florence), became widespread. Nevertheless, it took another full century until a perfect equilibrium between art and nature, as Alberti had recommended, was actually achieved.

By the end of the 16th century as Hauser writes, « the Pontifical State had assumed political hegemony over a divided Italy... The Curia as a financial power surpassed all the princes, lords, bankers, and merchants of Northern Italy; it could thus outdo them in pomp and in the field of art began to supplant Florence, which up to then had held the leading role... At this point arose that incomparable artistic activity... » a result of which was the development of the villa in grandiose and luxurious form. The villas as a group thus became an example of architecture defining a typology. The residence belonging to Cardinal Bessarione at Porta Capena is too tiny to be a precedent of any real importance and, on the other hand, the popes and high dignitaries had, up to that time, been entirely engrossed in other building projects such as St. Peter's and the restoration of the basilicas, while, at the same time, town planning problems in the cities had started to seriously emerge.

Of all the archaeological excavations of the day, the monuments which had the greatest influence with regard to classical Roman architecture were the « Domus Aurea » the « Orti degli Acilii, » the Palatine Hippodrome, and, most of all, the Sanctuary of Fortuna Primigenia at Palestrina. Their architectural features, together with the canons expressed in the literary tradition, influenced the layout of the Belvedere Court in the Vatican and the construction of Villa Madama on the slopes of Monte Mario.

The transformation of the old Belvedere of Innocent VIII and the pre-existing Vatican palace provided new models of space and perspective which were in part based upon the theories set forth by Alberti and Francesco di Giorgio Martini. This complex was in fact the work of an artist, Donato Bramante, who, in those years, as befit any

Bagnaia, Villa Lante: fresco of the loggia of the Palazzina Gambara showing the palace and the Villa Farnese at Caprarola (1587-1588. - A caryatid and a telamon figure frame the scene; in the middle the palace, with its unusual pentagonal plan, stands out before the gardens and the villa. Beyond the chestnut grove are the Cimini mountains.

self-respecting art lover, took a passionate interest in studying the Roman ruins. Likewise, in his design for the Villa Madama, Raphael, not only shows his ability to use architectural structures and forms in a most original manner, but also gives proof of his skill in « dominating the nature » of the site. His influence was Bramante in the Nymphaeum of Genazzano. For this reason, Villa Madama represents a fundamental milestone for typological studies on the villa. Baldassare Peruzzi, whose cultural background widely differed from Raphael's, created a kind of surburban dwelling hitherto unknown in Roman circles, i.e. the Farnesina Palace, which reveals Tuscan influence in both the garden and the overall harmony of the forms.

In short, all the hills in the immediate environs of Rome and the surrounding countryside were soon dotted with villas and gardens commissioned by famous families and cardinals for the express purpose of exalting either a certain personage or a whole family. The commissions represented a special aspect in the history of the villa dating back to the 15th century when it was a custom for the lords of the time to correspond about their architectural ventures, expressing or requesting opinions, and even going so far as to trade artists and architects.

16th century Rome witnessed the construction of the Orti of Paolo III Farnese (1534-1549) on the Palatine Hill, the huge villa of Julius III beyond the Porta del Popolo which, on account of its great size, represented the stage of passing from the 16th to 17th centuries, and, in the Vatican, the Casino of Pius IV built by Pirro Ligorio (1558-1561). Yet it was the Quirinal Hill which became the most famous of all. Of the villas built on the Quirinal, we shall mention the one belonging to Cardinal Carafa in which his entourage resided and which Pope Paul III of the Farnese family frequently visited. Enlarged and adorned starting in 1559 thanks to Ippolito d'Este, the so-called « Cardinal from Ferrara, » the villa's numerous gardens were filled with various plants, barrel-shaped pergolas, statuary, and wooden structures, thus constituting, along with works by Gerolamo da Carpi and Giovanni Alberto Galvani, a precursor of the gardens of Villa d'Este.

The villas were conceived as delightful spots for retreats, especially designed, as were the palaces, to provide their owners with luxurious living. They were often huge complexes with sumptuous rooms, looking out upon well-groomed parks containing gardens, fountains, statues, and aviaries.

In addition to the artistry of the architectural gardeners, the Cinquecento garden required, more than anything else, the contribution of an architect with his vision of harmonious regularity. The terrain to be worked on was taken just as it was, i.e. the various degrees of unevenness were used as topographical elements to be fitted into the overall pattern,

Obstacles such as uneven surfaces were once more overcome by means of terracing and wide-tread staircases, as the effect of monotony stemming from such solutions could easily be avoided by putting in fountains, flowerbeds, and small lawns. The entrances to the gardens consisted of gates which allowed the visitor to take in at a glance the villa and the park, or vice versa, according to the position of the whole complex in relation to the overall symmetry. The pathways, lined with cypress or pine trees, or else with holmoaks, box, juniper, and laurustine, were broken up by bas-reliefs, busts of famous men, or columns. Also, here and there at the intersections of the squared off hedges, there might be two-faced hermes and caryatids holding vases. Sculptures depicting every kind of mythological subject were employed as fountain ornaments, at first still in accordance with Quattrocento taste, i.e. as different kinds of modelled and carved shafts upon which the basins rested. The love for water was expressed in the most disparate ways, such as grottos, canals, fish pools, « scherzi d'acqua » (water games). It was employed all over; water was used in the same way as plants, i.e. it was considered something to be modelled as one wished.

It is thus the ancient Roman conception of the harmony binding beauty and nature which underlies the 16th century ideal of the villa. The villa represents a striving to achieve this harmony, yet before the Villa d'Este in Tivoli was built between 1550 and 1569, all these attempts had failed. Villa d'Este, the most complete model of garden landscaping, pointed out the artistic ideal to follow in order to attain that originality which throughout the Quattrocento artists had sought to create. And as a result of its uniqueness, its fame was carried down to the time of the construction of Versailles (1661). The flurry of admiration for the new Italian architectural gardening stemmed from the extraordinary blending of nature's multiple manifestations to architecture. And not only nature and architecture but also nature and sculpture, since water for the first time was treated as architecture (thanks to the use of newly-invented devices). The gardens embody the joining of the Humanistic culture of Ippolito d'Este to the archaeological passion of Pirro Ligorio. Ligorio was able to use just the proper dose of classical, i.e. in the planimetric and axial layout of the whole complex, while at the same time secking to reach a personal idealization of Nature.

Ligorio's design strongly influenced the villas of Caprarola and Lante of Bagnaia (1566-1578) which were being built at the time by several artists who had also worked on Villa d'Este. They reveal a common use of allegorical themes, both on the inside and in the architectural and geometric garden landscaping.

ANTONIO VENDITTI

IPPOLITO D'ESTE

Ippolito d'Este and Alessandro Farnese were the last of the great Renaissance cardinals. D'Este was born in 1509, the son of Alfonso I d'Este, the third duke of Ferrara and Lucrezia Borgia, the daughter of Pope Alexander VI. Not being the eldest, he was unable to succeed his father as duke, and, as was often the case for younger sons, he was launched on an ecclesiastical career.

By the time he was ten years old, he had succeeded his uncle Ippolito I as archbishop of Milan and at the age of twenty-seven he was sent to the court of Francis I in France as ambassador of the d'Este family. At twenty-nine he was made a cardinal. Although his educational and cultural background was rooted in the highly-refined Ferrarese court, renowned as one of Italy's great political and cultural centers, the thirteen years he spent in France served to deepen his love of art and start him out in his career as patron of artists and writers. He commissioned the famous names of his day: Benvenuto Cellini, the goldsmith, turned out tiny masterpieces for his table and magni-

Chapel of the Cardinal: altar containing a copy of the Virgin of Reggio. This fresco, which is traditionally attributed to Livio Agresti (c. 1500 - c. 1580) was instead definitely painted during the time of Alessandro d'Este since the miracle which made the Virgin of Reggio famous only took place in 1596.

ficent gifts for his friends; Titian, Federico Zuccari, Gerolamo Muziano, and Livio Agresti painted for him; Pierluigi da Palestrina was commissioned to compose for him; and poets such as Ariosto and Torquato Tasso were constant guests in his home. Yet Ippolito's involvement went further than supporting the art and artists of his day; he also put together great collections of sculpture, antique inscriptions, and all kinds of art objects which he used to decorate his various residences. All of them had to reflect both his taste and noble rank, as well as be fitting surroundings for his numerous entourage which was actually nothing less than a royal court.

In his native city of Ferrara, Ippolito d'Este owned the palaces of San Francesco, Belfiore, and a part of the Palazzo Paradiso. In France, he had commissioned Sebastiano Serlio to build a delightful residence at Fountainbleau for use during his frequent stays there. In Rome he held a lifetime lease on the Palace of Monte Giordano which he had decorated by a host of artists who embellished it with such pomp that even the Romans were awed by it. He also rented a villa at

The « Council of the Gods » painted by Federico Zuccari in the center of the ceiling in the Hercules Room which follows the composition of a fresco of the same subject painted by Raphael in the Farnesina. Here, Hercules has been placed amidst the gods. His figure, inspired by the Belvedere torso in the Vatican, is the one with the back turned on the extreme lefthand side of the painting, with the attributes of the club and lion's skin. Beside him are: Bacchus crowned with grapeleaves, Apollo with his lyre, Mars and Venus with little Cupid in the middle. On the right we can pick out: Vulcan, Neptune with his trident, Jupiter with his thunderbolts and the eagle next to Juno. Behind are: Diana, Ceres crowned with ears of wheat, and Minerva.

Monte Cavallo which he fixed up and landscaped with a stupendous garden. This villa, restored and partially rebuilt in the 17th century, is today known as the Quirinal Palace.

In 1540, as he had been appointed to the privy council of Francis I, king of France and his great protector, he was awarded the Abbey of St. Medan of Soisson, and later the abbeys of Pontigny and Boibonne. Appointed cardinal of Lyons, he chose to abdicate in favor of Cardinal Tournon in exchange for other considerable benefits. He served as governor of Siena on behalf of France, legate a latere in Germany, administrator of the archbishoprics of Aix-Narbonne, and administrator of the bishoprics of Orléans, Maurienne, and other abbeys, all of which paid him lucrative prebends.

LIBERALITAS

NOBILITAS

Allegories of Liberality, Nobility, and Generosity, frescoed in the center of the ceiling of the first ground floor hall by pupils of Federico Zuccari.

When Francis I died, his successor Henry II chose to acknowledge Ippolito's great worth and, granting him both protection and friendship, reconfirmed him in all his numerous public offices. Ippolito therefore continued to sit on the king's privy council, many times displaying great skill as a political advisor as, for example, when he successfully negotiated in favor of the Farnese League in opposition to Charles V.

Yet Ippolito cherished even greater ambitions: he dreamed of being elected pope. For five consecutive conclaves, he did everything in his power to see his wish fulfilled, from handing out money to wielding his great political power. But most of all he played upon the enormous prestige of his family which was one of the most important in Italy as the d'Estes boasted popes among their relations and were friends of the kings of France whom they often represented before the Holy See. These personal ambitions of Ippolito coincided with the political objectives of the French king who repeatedly promised him the votes of the French cardinals in three consecutive conclaves (instead, Julius III in 1550, Marcellus II in 1553, and Paul IV in 1555 were elected). Later Pius IV (1559-1565) sent him to Paris to protect the rights and hegemony of the church there and his mission turned out to be a veritable triumph. Ippolito d'Este was considered the wealthiest cardinal and the cleverest, most skilled diplomat of his day and perhaps because of this he was never elected by the conclave. Documentary evidence is provided by two of his contemporaries, the ambassadors of Florence and Venice to Rome. The former writes, « The Cardinal from Ferrara is the noblest in family, wealth, and alliances; nobody in the College of Cardinals can equal him. Nevertheless, more than a handful charge him with being too proud. » The latter records, « He is judged the wisest and most experienced of all the cardinals. He has the most incredible degree of patience when dealing with some problem. Yet there are two things that harm him: he was born too important and is overly ambitious to be elected to the papal throne, as we have seen on various occasions: from this stems our fear that his head is filled with overly grandiose schemes. »

During the 1550 conclave, the College of Cardinals was divided into three factions: the French cardinals in favor of Ippolito, the Farnese faction backing Alessandro, and the faction of Cardinal Pole which was the largest of the three. Cardinal Pole, an Englishman and an extremely devout Catholic, was feared for his avowed desire to see reforms instituted at all levels. Disliked by the French king who opposed his election, he had often openly declared when Paul III was still alive that, should he be elected, he would make it obligatory for the bishops to reside in their bishoprics and would demand the presence of the cardinals in the Curia. In addition, it was his intention to abolish all of their privileges. Although he lacked only a single vote to be elected, he failed to obtain it. Thereafter, Cardinal Ippolito's supporters reached an agreement with the Farnese faction whereby they combined forces in favor of Giovanni Maria del Monte who, elected, took the name of Julius III and was the last of the great Renaissance popes. Julius, a month after his election, decided to show his gratitude to Cardinal Ippolito d'Este by appointing him governor of Tivoli and its territories for life. Actually, the governorship of Tivoli was not very much sought after, mainly on account of the unruliness of the local population. Cardinal Alessandro Farnese had in fact previously turned down a similar appointment, but Ippolito II d'Este decided to accept — he had some very definite objectives in mind, not least of which was the opportunity of enriching his collection of antiquities by exploring Hadrian's Villa and the countless

Cardinal Ippolito II d'Este, oil portrait painted by Giancarlo Alù from an original pen drawing of the 16th century.

other villas dotting the Tiburtine territory. From the very beginning of his taking office, he commissioned an archaeologist — or antiquarian, as archaeologists were then called — to work for him. The man he chose, Pirro Ligorio, was renowned as the best in the field.

Ippolito made his entry into Tivoli on September 9, 1550, and it was a veritable triumph. The Tiburtine chronicles tell us that he reached the outskirts of the town escorted by an entourage numbering eighty odd gentlemen including counts, marquis, bishops, and knights where he was welcomed by one hundred Tiburtine noblemen on horseback who escorted him to Porta Santa Croce. Here, while blank cannon shots were fired off, one hundred youths waving olive branches gaily greeted him before a triumphal arch entwined with laurel leaves and adorned with the coats-of-arms of the Pope, the Cardinal, and the Commune of Tivoli. Meanwhile, from a platform set up for the occasion, a Tiburtine youth, dressed as Tiburtus, the legendary founder of Tivoli, declaimed verses in his honor. Inside the city, as G. M. Zappi narrates, magistrates, bishops, and high-ranking citizens not only welcomed him with all due honor, but even provided him with a carriage drawn by Moorish slaves.

Despite all the honors and such a sumptuous welcome, the residence reserved for the Cardinal and his entourage hardly lived up to what Ippolito's tastes and habits demanded. The building was actually an old monastery which had belonged to the Benedictines until 1256 when Pope Alexander turned it over to the newborn Franciscan order.

15

Detail of the fresco by Gerolamo Muziano in the Audience Hall (1565-67) with a view of the villa and the gardens as they were originally designed.

As the Franciscans used only a tiny part of the building, the remainder had been turned into the official residence of the Governor-Cardinals. We learn from a letter sent by Ippolito to his brother, Ercole II, Duke of Ferrara, that after just a bit more than a month at Tivoli (from September 9 to October 28, 1550), Ippolito had regained his health, undermined by the stress of the conclave he had just attended, to such a degree that he had made up his mind to turn the monastery into a real villa. This may be considered the birth of the Villa d'Este.

THE VILLA

This marked the beginning of the period of buying up the land adjoining the monastery and the underlying terrain, the so-called « valle gaudente » (« joyous valley ») where the garden was to be. The plan was to enlarge and restructure the old monastery, but it was necessary to heed, in the building plan, the church of Santa Maria Maggiore and, in the garden layout, the church of St. Peter's. In fact, on the far side of the courtyard of the building was—and still is—one of Santa Maria Maggiore's side walls and the garden tapers off below by the church of St. Peter's. Evidently not even Cardinal Ippolito was able to expropriate and demolish two important church buildings. Consequently, since building over a pre-existing structure could not be avoided — and indeed some of the old walls had to be utilized — the planimetric pattern of the building turned out to be irregular.

Work was begun right after the cardinal's stay at Tivoli, although it was interrupted again and again, partially due to the fact that Ippolito, by order of Henry II (1551), left almost immediately for Siena. Only during the summer of 1555 did he return to Tivoli, and then just for a brief visit since in December of that year the new pope Paul IV had convicted him of simony and divested him of the office of Governor of Tivoli, sending him off to Lombardy. In 1560, just after the death of Paul IV and the election of Pius IV, Cardinal Ippolito was once more appointed governor of the Tiburtine territories for life, and so he went off to spend the summer at Tivoli. From then on his stays became frequent and regular. This was undoubtedly the period that work was once more undertaken at full speed and perhaps the considerable changes wrought on the original plans to reconstruct the building date back to this time. Nonetheless, the project was held up once more during the reign of Pope Pius V (1568) when, as a result of the new relationships that had grown up between monarchs and the Church, Cardinal Ippolito was destituted of all his lucrative French offices.

The differences between the original plans and what was actually partially put up later may be seen by comparing a painting by Muziano dated c. 1565 with an engraving by Dupérac of 1573. The two building stages are visible even in the façade which, albeit unfinished, reveals the use of different kinds of building materials, i.e. stucco and travertine. Even a superficial examination shows that a number of structures are missing from the two upper floors, the protruding wings are not completely finished (in fact, they were to end in a tower-shaped top floor), and the corners and footing lack the planned ashlar-work covering. Yet the appearance of the façade is simple and luminous, and the slight protrusion of the wings provides greater emphasis to the double loggia of the central section joining the two halves of the main staircase. This double loggia serves the two most important floors of the building, i.e. the Cardinal's suite and the floor used for official ceremonies. The top floor (with the Cardinal's rooms) provides a panoramic view, while the floor below opens out on a perspective view of the underlying garden.

The main section of the building takes up two floors, i.e. courtyard level where the Cardinal's rooms were located, and the floor beneath with the reception halls and the great hall with the fountain. In the rear was a long cryptoporticus, partially covered with mosaic and stucco designs which are reminiscent of Hadrian's Villa. The decoration of the rooms on these floors was carried out by a team of painters, stucco workers, and *fontanieri* (fountain workers) who worked closely together following a carefully set out iconographic scheme to complete the symbolism of the garden. The Cardinal's suite on the portico level was originally supposed to be adorned with sixteen tapestries portraying the story of the mythological Hippolytus [1], but Pirro Ligorio, who had received the commission for the project, only came up with a description and sketches [2]. Painted along the friezes in the central hall were several female figures personifying Wisdom, Humanity, Charity, and Patience. Two other rooms were decorated with other Virtues and eight busts of Greek philosophers

---

[1] Hippolytus, son of the Athenese hero Theseus and the queen of the Amazons Hippolyte, greatly loved hunting and chastity and thus honored Diana. Venus, jealous of this, caused his stepmother Phedra, third wife of Theseus, to fall passionately in love with him. But Hippolytus rejected her and Phedra filled her husband's ears with tales about him so that Theseus prayed Neptune to punish his son for him. Thus, one day while Hippolytus was driving his chariot along the beach, a monster emerged from the water frightening the horses who crashed the chariot and Hippolytus, dragged over the rocks, met a horrible death. Then Esculapius upon the intercession of Diana brought him back to life. Diana, in order to hide him from Jupiter, who was angered at seeing his power usurped, brought him to Aricia in Latium, where he lived under the name of Virbius (Ovid, Metamorphoses, XV, v. 492).

[2] The description of these tapestries, written in Ligorio's own handwriting, has come down to us and is preserved in the Morgan Library in New York. The manuscript is made up of 19 folios in which Ligorio divides the story of Hippolytus-Virbius into sixteen parts, each of which is illustrated by a drawing. Each of these drawings was to have been made into a tapestry.

Overall view of Muziano's fresco.

by pupils of Federico Zuccari. Stucco decorations and paintings by Livio Agresti embellished the chapel.

On the ceiling of the downstairs audience hall Federico Zuccari painted a Banquet of the Gods set in a mock perspective of columns and, in the corner medallions, allegories of the Four Seasons. The wall paintings were frescoed by Gerolamo Muziano and his pupils in April 1565. Their iconographic scheme has to do with geographic symbolism: from the wall with the fountain portraying the circular temple of Sibyl and its imitation waterfall (an attempt to represent the Tivoli of Antiquity) to the depictions of the Cardinal's holdings in Rome (the Quirinal Palace) and in Tivoli (the Villa d'Este and the Organ and Oval Fountains). Dominating the whole is the d'Este eagle protecting the golden apples of the Hesperides, from whence derives the Cardinal's motto: « ab insomni non custodita dracone. »

The other rooms are decorated with scenes of the battle of Tiburtus and Catillus against the Latins, the foundation of Tibur and the sacrifices related to this event, and the battle of Hercules Saxanus, on his way back with Geryon's cattle and the Hesperides' golden apples, against Albio and Belgio. Next is the room which has a ceiling fresco depicting the drowning of King Anius in the river Parensius which was henceforth known as the river Aniene, the chariots of Apollo and Venus drawn by dolphins, and, lastly, the rooms with the sacrifice of Noah after the Flood and the miracle of Moses causing water to spring from a rock (the latter being a clear reference to Cardinal Ippolito and his fountains). The scarcity of Christian themes has been remarked upon. It is almost as if the Cardinal wanted to show that he was above all a Renaissance prince who had hardly been touched by the new spirit of the Counter-Reformation even though the pagan subjects he chose clearly exalt Christian virtues.

18

Banquet of the Gods framed by a perspective of mock columns. It was painted by Zuccari and his pupils, probably around 1567 in the center of the ceiling of the Audience Hall.

Above: fountain located along a wall of the Audience Hall. It was begun by the fountaineer Curzio Maccarone and finished by Paolo Calandrino from Bologna in 1568. It represents the artist's conception of Tivoli in Antiquity with the Temple of the Siblys and the Aniene Cascades. - Righthand page, above: Venus on the seashell drawn by a dolphin who was responsible for Neptune's turning Ino and her child Melicerta into the seagods Leucothe and Palemon after they had been drowned. The fresco was painted around 1569 on a wall of the second Tiburtine room, almost certainly by Cesare Nebbia. - Below: Apollo personifying the Sun on his sun chariot, painted in the center of the ceiling of the second Tiburtine room by Cesare Nebbia in around 1569.

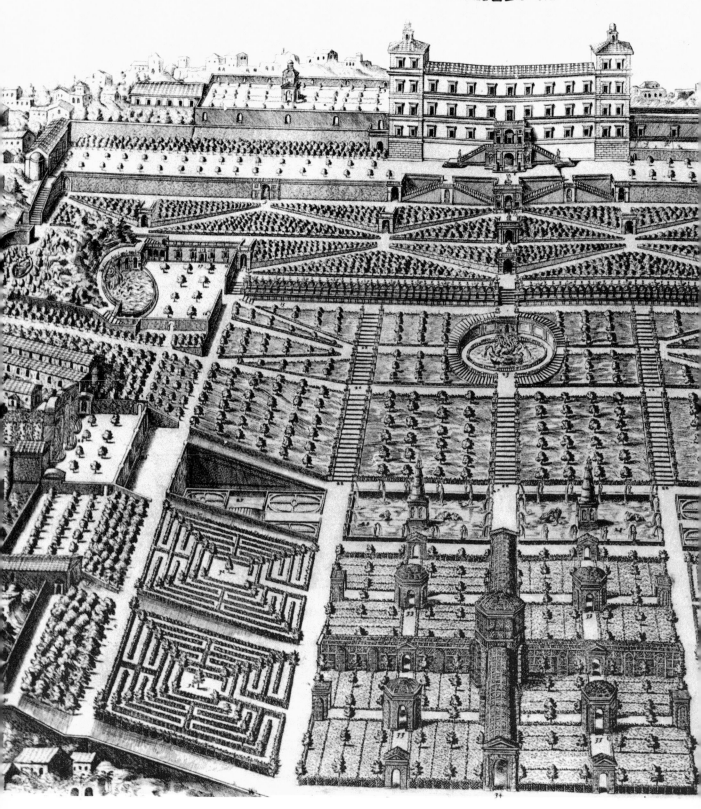

TO HER MOST CHRISTIAN MAJESTY CATERINA DE' MEDICI, MOTHER OF HIS MOST CHRISTIAN MAJESTY CHARLES IX KING OF FRANCE

Such was the renown of the sumptuous palace and the exquisite gardens ordered by the illustrious Cardinal from Ferrara, Hippolito, in the city of Tivoli that the all-mighty Emperor Maximilian wanted to obtain a drawing of it, as an example of the most perfect of its kind, even in comparison to those built in Antiquity. He desired that I be the one to make the aforesaid drawing and I longed to dedicate it to Her Majesty since I was aware of how the Cardinal during his lifetime was her devoted and affectionate servant and how she loved beautiful buildings and pleasant gardens. I pray that she kindly deigns to accept this little gift, and myself among her subjects and servants. With this prayer I humbly stoop to kiss her royal hand, praying that God preserve her in her happiness.
Rome, 8th day of April 1573.
Your humble subject and servant, Étienne Dupérac, Parisian.

TO THOSE WHO LOVE AND DELIGHT IN SEEING LOVELY AND RARE THINGS BY ANTONIO LAFRERJ

Greatly admirable is the site of the city of Tivoli where one can see how the course of the river Aniene, furiously storming down the mountains of Latium, has created inside the stone veins stupendous furrows and grottos which, with the passing of time and on account of its nature, has generated mineral deposits of various shapes so that in many places, frozen, these appear to be human figures or else animals, fruits, or other stupendous objects. Taking this into consideration, the illustrious Cardinal from Ferrara decided to alter the course of the waters and build an exquisite palace and garden, through which he caused the waters to flow, so that in the palace and in the garden there are lovely fountains as embellishment with miniature forests, labyrinths, herb gardens, and many other things which cannot be shown in drawings, since a huge volume would be necessary to show all of them. But following my love of perfection, I printed and annotated the most notable things to be seen so that all those who delight in such things may enjoy such a remarkable work.
1. The palace, the decoration of the palace, and the fountain inside it cannot be described herein. 2. The secret garden. 3. The Unicorn Fountain. 4. Pavilion with four fountains from which water spouts. 5. Tennis court. 6. Palace stairs and in the center the Fountain of Leda. 7. The Fountain of Thetis 8. Two fountains of Esculapius and Hygeia. 9. The Fountain of Arethusa. 10. The Fountain of Pandora. 11. The Fountain of Pomona. 12. The Fountain of Flora. 13. Pathway which crosses the whole garden along which there are three water pipes, one above the other, from which water spouts in different ways whereby creating wonderful effects. 14. The great fountain on top of which there are three colossals; one of the Sibyl Albunea with her son Melicertes, the others of the two rivers, the Ercolaneo and the Aniene; all of which spout water into three huge basins that is then collected in the basin of a huge oval vase around which are ten nymphs holding urns from which water constantly pours, it too into the same vase. 15. The Fountain of Pegasus. 16. Two fountains of Bacchus. 17. Grotto of Venus, inside of which there is a fountain with a Venus in the center and on the sides four nude cupids who are pouring water from four vases. 18. Grotto of Diana, inside of which there are two fountains, one of Diana, the other of Pallas, with many other statues and exquisite mosaic decorations. 19. Large fountain representing Rome with the seven hills, aqueducts, temples, statues, and other embellishments, and on every side delightful fountains. 20. Fountain of the Emperors. 21. The Fountain of the Birds, which has numerous songbirds perched on bronze branches, who sing in their natural voices by means of the water. Then, as soon as an Owl, it too of bronze, appears, the birds stop singing and the owl starts to hoot. 22. Travertine stairs with bannisters on either side and plinths above each one from which spout jets of water in the form of vapor. 23. The Fountain of the Dragons with a jet of water which shooting into the air makes a noice like cannon fire. 24. The Fountain of the Goddess Nature. This fountain well deserves its nickname of fountian of marvels. Here an organ with admirable art, driven by the waters, plays by itself any madrigal tune one desires in four or five voices. There are many other things even more stupendous — I have not yet finished. 25. Grottos of the Sibyls. 26. Fountain of Antinous. 27. Fishponds divided into compartments. 28. Fishponds with conical spouts in the center imperceptibly exuding water. 29. Fountain of Neptune with a depiction of the god Oceanus. 30. Fountain of the Venus Cloacina. 31. The Fountain of Triton. 32. Labyrinths. 33. Herb garden. 34. The entranceway to the garden, which is not on the drawing, with two circles and two rustic fountains. 35. Lakes beyond the garden boundaries.

23

Oval in the second Tiburtine room in which the legendary king Anius is depicted. During
a desperate attempt to catch his daughter Cloris kidnapped by Mercury, King Anius drowned
in the river Parensius which thereafter was called Aniene after him.

THE GARDEN

The garden of the Villa d'Este was essentially conceived in architectural terms, and its symbolism developed so that it could be easily deciphered by any erudite Renaissance gentleman. The garden is laid out upon a steep slope which, viewed from the building, descends to the terrace below by means of a series of ramps and pathways. Yet we should try to imagine the original viewpoint that generally was from the lower level entrance, as a person coming from Rome would usually enter the villa from a sideroad off the Via Tiburtina. From this entrance, the main axis cutting through the pools

comes out at the Fountain of the Dragons which marks the start of the steeper zone and thereafter leads to the main staircase of the double loggia and right into the center of the great underlying terrace. Four transversal axes branch out of the great terrace: one called the Cardinal's Path; a second which starts out at the Oval Fountain and crosses the Hundred Fountains Path, ending at the fountain of Rome; the third, the Hydrangea Path, leading to the Fountain of the Dragons and the Fountain of the Owl; and the fourth which, from the Organ Fountain, skirting the fishponds, was supposed to end

Detail of the fresco by Muziano in the Audience Hall showing the lower section of the garden.

at the Fountain of Neptune but never went beyond the design stage. This latter cross-axis divides the hilly part from the flatter land before the gate. Originally there was a traditional garden bordering the labyrinths here, which was enclosed inside a garden wall. Wooden trellises covered with grapevines and square-shaped zones bordered by fruit trees and planted with aromatic herbs gave the garden a cross-shaped pattern. In the center stood an octagonal pavilion with three silver eagles and the gilded fleur-de-lis of the House of d'Este dominating the cornice; four fountains in the shape of flowers were set around it. Today the so-called Rotunda is what remains of this.

To see the actual architectonic garden, one had to leave this first section. The architectonic garden in fact starts out at the level of the fishponds, of which, according to the original plan, there were

supposed to be four (the one on the side of the Organ Fountain was never built); the fishponds were bounded on one side by the slope on top of which was the Organ Fountain. On the opposite side there was to be a fountain symbolizing the sea, depicting Neptune atop a chariot drawn by seahorses, which was never built.

The Organ Fountain was begun in 1568 by a certain Luca Clerico and Claude Venard. The four travertine hermes with their arms crossed are by Pirrino de' Gagliardo. The center niche contains a copy of an antique statue of Diana of Ephesus preserved in the Farnese collection (now at the end of the garden) which was executed by a Flemish artist, Gillis van den Vliete. According to the Paris Manuscript there were to have been statues of Diana and Apollo at either side, but the façade was finished in the Baroque style only towards 1611 by

Above: engraving by Venturini (1685) with a view of the so-called Rotunda of the Cypresses located in the lower section of the garden. - Below: centuries old cypresses in the Rotunda.

Cardinal Alessandro d'Este who had it crowned with the d'Este eagle, after removing the statue of Diana. Cardinal Alessando is also responsible for the « tempietto » which protects the organ inserted into the central niche and he also had the statues of Apollo and Orpheus placed on either side. Claude Venard is credited with having built the water organ based upon models from Antiquity known during the Renaissance through the descriptions of Vitruvius and Hero of Alexandria. However, the Villa d'Este organ was quite a wonder in itself since, compared to the antique models, it was highly perfected and it was also wholly autonomous. The operating principle is very simple: water powerfully rushing into a cavity forced air out of the organ pipes while another water-driven device simultaneously moved the keys whereby generating a harmonious sound preceded by a trumpet call. The Tiburtine chronicles

Above: fresco in the Audience Hall, perhaps repainted in the time of Cardinal Rinaldo I
(1641-1672) showing a view of the fishponds and the cascades of the Organ Fountain. -
On the right: the Organ Fountain with its waterfall, the modern fountain of Neptune (1927)
and a partial view of the fishponds.

Engraving by Venturini (1685): front view of the Organ Fountain.

narrate that when Pope Gregory XIII paid a visit to the villa in September of 1573, he was so impressed with sound of this organ that he insisted on congratulating the artist responsible for it in person.

In 1566 excavations for the four pools got underway. The pool beneath the Organ Fountain was begun and never finished, just as the grotto beneath the fountain that was supposed to contain the sibyls (eight antique statues) and the Fountain of Antinous, which was to be right by the pool and act as its background.

In 1611 a part of the giant group with Neptune which had been begun for the fountain on the opposite side was placed under the huge cascade of the Organ Fountain. Here in 1927 the modern fountain of Neptune was set up. Along the second transversal axis, in the center, is the Fountain of the Dragons which, the chroniclers of the 16th century tell us, was built in a single night for the visit of Gregory XIII whose family coat-of-arms contained

a dragon (³). This chronicle-legend has been disproved by documents (see the Paris Manuscript) which report that the fountain was designed even before the election of Gregory XIII. In the middle of the huge basin four giant dragon heads spit water while amidst them a powerful jet spurts forth. The jet used to be turned off and on to create explosion noises. Alongside the fountain are two staircases winding around the fountain itself and on the railings two little graded canals from which the water de-

(³) This fountain is now commonly known as the Fountain of the Dragons, but it would be more appropriate to call it the Fountain of the Dragon. In fact, what appears to be four dragons in the center of the basin are actually four of the hundred heads of Ladonis, the monster who helped the Hesperides to watch over the golden apples. This is confirmed in the Paris Manuscript which describes the fountain as follows: « It is called the Fountain of the Dragon because it shows the famous Dragon who guarded the Garden of the Hesperides. As the ancient texts recount, the dragon has one hundred heads, and from each mouth spouts water into a huge fishpond. »

Present-day front of the Organ Fountain (night view).

Engraving by Venturini (1685): cascade of the Organ Fountain (executed by G. L. Bernini in 1661).

scends in tiny waves. The large niche in the back once contained a statue of Hercules.

On the same transversal axis looking right from the Fountain of the Dragons is the Fountain of the Owl. We hardly know anything about when the project was begun, although we do know the name of the person who started it (Giovanni del Duca) and the person who continued work on it when del Duca died c. 1566 (Raffaello Sangallo). In 1568 Ulisse Macciolini completed the stucco statues depicting three fauns. In 1572 Leonardo Sormanno carved eight satyr figures each of which was holding a vase with water flowing out of them, for the niches in the wall bordering the fountain. In the middle is the great niche flanked by two columns decorated with a mosaic design of grapevines and golden apples of the Garden of the Hesperides and surmounted by two female figures; in the center above the niche, two angels support the Cardinal's shield with an eagle and fleur-de-lis

design. Unfortunately, the most original part of the fountain, which in its day roused endless wonder, is no longer extant: the middle section, made up of three statues of youths seated upon a huge vase out of which water poured into the basin below. In the fake rock used as the niche background and support for the vase were delicate branches made of bronze upon which birds were perched. Using the same principle as the water organ, the birds were made to chirp. Their song would stop only when an owl, again powered by a water device, appeared and started to hoot lugubriously.

By the Fountain of the Owl is the fountain usually known today as Proserpine. Bounded by a wall with niches and two lateral staircases leading to an upper level; it was originally known as the Fountain of

Fountain of the Dragons.

Engraving by Venturini (1685): Fountain of the Dragons, also known as the Fountain of the Wheel.

the Emperors, having been named after the statues, no longer extant, of the four emperors who had built villas on Tiburtine territory, which originally decorated the niches. Alongside the huge and extremely deep niche hollow are four twisted columns covered with a grapevine pattern inspired by the Constantinian basilica of St. Peter's. According to the original plans, statues of Arethusa and two other nymphs (never sculpted) were to have gone in the niche. In the 17th century a stucco group of Pluto and Proserpine was instead set up here and hence the name of the fountain which serves as background for an open-air dining space.

Not far from the Fountain of the Owl is another remarkable complex known as the « Bollori » (« Boilers »). It acts as a stairway leading to the upper level. Upon the plinth of the parapets are forty-two low water jets which give the impression of emitting

boiling water. The fountain was deemed « the villa's finest water view, » by Vincenzo Vincenzi, a master fountaineer of the 17th century.

On the third transversal axis we reach the fountains judged the villa's most important and perhaps, according to what the chroniclers of the day have left us, the most important in Italy. To the left, facing the palace, is the Fountain of Tivoli or the Oval Fountain, as it has been called ever since 1576 by the historian Zappi. The great waterfall alludes to the famous Tivoli cascades, the grottos to the mountains of Tivoli, and the statues placed inside it to the three rivers flowing through the Tiburtine territory (the Aniene, the Albuneo, and the Erculaneo). In the area of the fountain were two statues depicting Bacchus, representing the story of the god who was raised by a nymph, sister to his mother, Semele, when Semele was struck by one of Jupiter's

Detail of the fresco by Muziano in the Audience Hall with the Fountain of the Dragons and the niche containing the colossal statue of Hercules.

Engraving by Venturini (1685): Fountain of the Owl. It is interesting to see the numerous « scherzi d'acqua » (water games) of the fountain.

thunderbolts (⁴). Behind the mock mountain is a statue of the mythological winged horse, Pegasus, creating a parallel between the mountain of Tivoli and Mt. Parnassus, the mountain of the Muses. Upon Mt. Parnassus was the celebrated fountain of Hippocrene (from the Greek, spring of horses) which had supposedly been created from the blow of one of Pegasus's hoofs as he took off in flight. Set inside the huge niches in the semicircle were ten statues of nymphs designed by Pirro Ligorio and sculpted by G. Della Porta. Within the fountain boundaries, to the right, are entrances leading to a three-part grotto, today bare, known as the « Grotto of Venus. » The main fountain of the grotto was decorated with a statue of Venus leaving her bath, very much like the Capitoline Venus, next to which were two cupids, one of which was holding a goose

by the neck while the other was astride a goose. Upon the edge of the fountain basin were four more naked cupids bearing upon their shoulders a vase out of which water gushed. It would seem that the other two sections of the grotto, since they were kept bare, were used as storerooms for statuary awaiting final destination, such as the two Hercules statues which were placed one behind the other above the Fountain of the Dragons. From the Tivoli-Oval Fountain to the Fountain of Rome (today known as Rometta) extends the Path of the Hundred Fountains containing twenty-two fountains in the shape of a boat, alternating with obelisks and eagles and the fleur-de-lis of the d'Este family, fed by three canals with hundreds of tiny spouts The glazed terracotta decoration with high reliefs depicting Ovid's Metamorphoses is no longer extant (⁵).

(⁴) There were two statues of Bacchus to symbolize the double birth of this god, son of Jupiter and Semele. In fact, Bacchus' mother died before he was even born since, egged on by Juno in a jealous rage, Jupiter, to show off his great might, had struck her down dead. Then Jupiter, who wanted to save the unborn child, had him removed from his mother's womb and sewn up inside his thigh, whereby he was able to bring the pregnancy to full term. When the time came, the child was born and Jupiter entrusted him to the care of Semele's sister, Ino. Ino lovingly raised her nephew. This aroused such a rage in Juno that she caused Ino to go crazy and throw herself

into the sea, whereupon Ino was turned into the seagoddess Leucothe (Ovid, Metamorphoses, IV, v. 481). Ino was identified by the Romans as the Mater Matuta whom Livius also identified as Albunea, the Tiburtine sibyl.

(⁵) The 91 terracotta plaques with scenes from Ovid's Metamorphoses have practically all been lost and those extant are unfortunately covered over by maidenhair fern. The fifteen books of the *Metamorphoses* by Publius Ovid Naso, which was a simple, clearly written compendium of all Greek and Roman mythology, served as the main source for the palace and garden decoration.

The Fountain of the Owl as it looks today without the complicated device for which it was named.

Engraving by Venturini (1685): the Fountain of Prosperine, formerly the Emperors' Fountain, since in the open-air dining space which made up its background, there were originally statues of the four Roman emperors who had built villas in the environs of Tivoli, i.e. Caesar, Augustus, Trajan, and Hadrian. The central niche of this fountain was to have held statues of Arethusa and two other nymphs, but they were never carved. Then in the 17th century the stucco group of Pluto and Proserpine (which caused the name of the fountain to be changed) was set up here.

The Fountain of Rome or Rometta rises upon a platform and symbolizes both Tivoli and Rome; in fact, the water descends as a fall to represent the Tivoli cascades, while at the same time a stucco statue of a rivergod holds up the Temple of the Sibyl; still farther below a statue portraying the Appennines is borne by the River Aniene. The water flows into the Tiber which has a boat in the middle to symbolize the Tiberine Islet. The boat itself has an obelisk for a mast to recall the Temple of Esculapius. On the platform stood the decorated part of the fountain begun in 1568 by the fountaineer Curzio Maccarone. It was semi-circular in shape and represented the Seven Hills of Rome and their major monuments; the hills were joined together by archways which, separately, represented the triumphal arches and, together, the Claudian Aqueduct. According to Zappi (1576), it was possible to pick out the Colosseum, the Septizonius of Septimius Severius, the Pantheon, etc. This fountain, the work

of the Cardinal's archaeologist, Pirro Ligorio, still has the statue of Rome in the middle of its vast semi-circle. The statue was carved, after a design by Ligorio, by the Flemish sculptor, Pierre de la Motte. De la Motte is also responsible for the group of the She-wolf and Remus and Romulus. The group with a horse being attacked by a lion representing the struggle between Rome (the lion) and Tivoli (the horse), was added opposite the statue of the Wolf and twins in c. 1607.

This extraordinary fountain (without a basin to collect the water which flows at the base of the podium, and thus reminiscent of the Tiber) was used as a theater; the hemispherical layout of the small reconstructions of monuments in back of the podium creates a spatial area like that of the pits of Renaissance theaters. It should also be remembered that theater was one of the Cardinal's favorite pastimes and that his friend, the erudite French Humanist Marc-Antoine Muret used to write plays

Fountain of Proserpine (night view).

Engraving by Venturini (1685): the staircase known as « Bollori ».

for him and his friends. On the other hand, in the Paris Manuscript examined by Coffin, it was specifically stated that the platform was supposed to be used as an open-air dining loggia. The ramps at the end of the Path of the Hundred Fountains led to the upper level just below the terrace of the villa. This transversal axis which runs the whole breadth of the garden was called the Cardinal's Path because the Cardinal and his friends used to converse as they walked up and down it.

To the northeast was the grotto of Esculapius [6] and Hygeia: the statues of the two deities are now respectively in the Louvre and the Vatican. In the center is the delightful loggia completed c. 1570 which, in addition to providing access to the stairs leading to the terrace, also encompasses three niches

containing antique statues: a Pandora [7], a Minerva (now in the Capitoline Museum), and a third whose identity is unknown.

At the end of the « Cardinal's Path » is the Grotto of Diana, perhaps the most elaborately decorated of the grottos: the flooring is paved in majolica with designs of fleur-de-lis, golden apples, and the eagles from the coat-of-arms of the d'Este family, at the corners were stucco reliefs with female figures holding baskets full of golden apples, and the floor

[6] This grotto at Villa d'Este was most likely dedicated to Esculapius for his connection to the myth of Hippolytus (It was Esculapius who brought Hippolytus back to life).

[7] Pandora (in Greek = all the gifts) was the first woman and received gifts from all the gods. Jupiter, angry with Prometheus who had stolen fire from the heavens to give it to mankind, gave her a box to present to Prometheus but he, fearing a trick, refused to accept it. Prometheus' brother, Epimetheus, fell in love with Pandora and wed her. One day, curious to see what was inside the box, she opened it and all the various kinds of evil escaped and fell upon the earth. Remaining on the bottom of the box, there was only hope. Parallels have often been drawn between Pandora and Eve.

40

Above: the Staircase of the « Bollori ». -
To the right: the mythological winged
horse Pegasus born from the blood of
the decapitated Medusa was carved in
travertine by Gillis van den Vliete and
placed on the top of the artificial mountain which represents the mountains of
Tivoli in the Oval Fountain. Just as
Pegasus's flight from Mount Helicon
caused the spring of Hippocrene (sacred to the Muses) to gush forth, this
point marks the origin of the Tiburtine
rivers.

Engraving by Venturini (1685): Fountain of Tivoli, which has been called the Oval Fountain ever since 1576 because of its oval shape. Taken as a whole it symbolizes the city of Tivoli with its waterfall, rivers, mountains, and the Sibyl Albunea.

Fresco on one of the walls of the first Tiburtine room with the Oval Fountain as it was being built. This is further documentary proof for the dating of the frescoes in this and the adjoining rooms of 1569.

Tivoli or Oval Fountain.

Statue of the Sibyl Albunea with a child, probably Melicerta, the son of the nymph Ino, who was turned into the sea-goddess Leucothe. Albunea was likened by the Romans to the Tiburtine Sibyl. The sculpture stands in the middle of the artificial rocks on the Fountain of Tivoli (Oval), and was carved in travertine by Gillis van den Vliete after a drawing by Ligorio.

Statues of the two Tiburtine rivers, the Ercolaneo and the Aniene in the two grottos on either side of the Sibyl. Above: engraving by Venturini (1685): Pathway of Albunea (which symbolizes the third river, the Albuneo) probably carved by Giovanni Malanca in 1566.

designs were repeated in stucco on the ceiling. The walls were decorated with stucco bas-reliefs depicting Perseus and Andromeda ([8]), Diana and Acteon ([9]), Apollo and Daphne ([10]), Pan and Syrinx ([11]), and Diana and Callisto ([12]). This remarkable decorative scheme served to set off the famous statues now in the Capitoline Museum: the Amazon, Lucretia of Rome, Minerva, and the Diana with her bow and faithful dog which gave the grotto its name.

Above the Grotto of Diana was another open-air dining space with four niches for statues symbolizing the Four Seasons sculpted out of peperino. On either side of the entrance, by the terrace, were the antique statues of Bacchus and Mars now in the Ince Blundell Hall Collection in England. Opposite this « dining hall » is the fountain named for Thetis, the mother of Achilles. Lastly, at the center, beneath the loggia, is the Fountain of Leda which contained three niches with antique statues: the Leda and the Swan now in the Borghese Museum and Helen and Clytemnestra. In front of the loggia is the Fountain of the Seahorses, consisting of an antique tripod with three seahorses (no longer extant) which came from Hadrian's Villa.

To complete the west side of the villa a court for ball games had been marked out on one side, while on the other was a secret garden where the statue of Venus, now in the courtyard, once stood.

([8]) Andromeda, the beautiful daughter of Cepheus, king of Ethiopia, was to be sacrificed to a sea monster, but was saved by Perseus. Perseus riding his winged horse Pegasus, slew the monster and freed Andromeda who he then wed (Ovid, Metamorphoses, IV, v. 683).

([9]) Acteon was a skilled hunter who was turned into a deer by Diana and torn to pieces by her dogs because he had caught a glimpse of her bathing in the Parthenia fountain (Ovid, Metamorphoses, III, v. 138).

([10]) The nymph Daphne, pursued by Apollo who loved her with unrequited love, prayed to be turned into a laurel plant to escape him. Her wish was fulfilled and laurel became the plant Apollo held sacred (Ovid, Metamorphoses, I, v. 452).

([11]) Pan was a god of nature and forests, half man and half goat, who protected shepherds and hunters. He fell in love with Syrinx, a nymph from Arcadia, who did not return his love. Pan pursued her until she invoked her father Ladonis to turn her into a reed. Her father granted her wish whereupon Pan cut the reed and made it into the instrument he called a « syrinx » (Ovid, Metamorphoses, I, v. 680).

By the time Cardinal Ippolito met his death on December 2, 1572 ([13]), the general layout of the gardens had already been completed, even though only a few of the fountains were at the time finished. The completion of the architecture was left to his successors who, aside from a few slight modifications, faithfully carried out the original plans.

Cardinal Ippolito had willed the villa to cardinals of the House of d'Este and, should there be no heirs, to the deacon of the College of Cardinals. Cardinal Luigi d'Este (1538-1586) spent some time in Tivoli and when he died the villa passed into the hands of Deacon Alessandro Farnese. Work was again undertaken in 1605 when Cardinal Alessandro d'Este was appointed Governor of Italy. In 1621 he managed to have the will changed so that the villa became the exclusive property of the d'Este family. Other work was carried out during the time of Cardinal Rinaldo I d'Este (1633-1672). Bernini was commissioned first with the Fountain of the Bicchierone (« Big Goblet ») and then in 1611 with the cascade of the Organ Fountain. Later other projects were entrusted to a pupil of Bernini's, the architect Mattia de' Rossi, who in 1671 carried out several alterations to the palace and enriched the water show of the Fountain of Rome and the Fountain of the Dragons.

Villa d'Este was celebrated before it was even finished. We have proof in the frescoes of Caprarola and Bagnaia and in an engraving by Dupérac dedicated to Caterina de' Medici. The engraving was taken from a drawing commissioned by Maximilian of Austria who deemed the villa of such perfection that it could withstand comparison against any other in existence.

([12]) Callisto was a nymph and one of Diana's hunting companions. She had a child Arcas, the father of whom was Jupiter. Having failed to keep her vow of chastity she was cast off by Diana. Later she was turned into a bear by Juno and afterwards into a constellation by Jupiter (Ovid, Metamorphoses, II, v. 409).

([13]) Ippolito II died in Rome on December 2, 1572 in the palace of Monte Giordano after a brief illness. The funeral rite was solemnly celebrated in the church of Santa Maria in Aquiro of which he had been the titular cardinal. Marc-Antoine Muret delivered the funeral oration in his polished Latin. The Cardinal's remains were laid to rest in the church of San Francesco in Tivoli on December 8, 1572.

Pathway of the Hundred Fountains begun around 1569, which joins the two principal fountains of the villa, namely the Tivoli (Oval) and Rome (Rometta) fountains. Its name comes from the numerous spouts which stick out of tiny fountains, of different shapes such as boats, obelisks, eagles, and lilies. This complex, more than any other place in the villa, reveals the erudition of the person who thought it up. In fact, in the middle it was decorated with ninety-one terracotta high-reliefs depicting scenes taken from Ovid's Metamorphoses. At the same time, along with the two fountains at either end, it constituted one of the focal points of the geographic symbolism of the villa: the three little canals that it is made up of represent the three Tiburtine rivers (the Aniene, the Ercolaneo, and the Albuneo) which, starting at the Fountain of Tivoli, flow together to form the Tiber in the Rome Fountains. - To the left: a detail of Gerolamo Muziano's fresco depicting the Pathway of the Hundred Fountains.

The Pathway of the Hundred Fountains as it apperas today, with very little left of the terracotta panels and practically all overgrown with maidenhair fern and moss.

Engraving by Venturini (1685): the Fountain of Rome, constructed on a semi-circular platform, presents the monuments of Antique Rome in miniature. At either side are two medieval gates, the Flaminia and the San Paolo. In the center, behind the statue of Rome carved by Pierre de La Motte, the Pantheon may be made out. In addition other monuments can be seen, such as the Colosseum, the Septizonium of Septimius Severus, the columns of Trajan and Marcus Aurelius, the Temple of Murcia and the Temple of Victory, and the triumphal arches of Septimius Severus, Titus, and Constantine. Besides serving to link up the hills of Rome, these arches were meant to represent the Aqueduct of Claudius. The water lapping on the platform symbolizes the Tiber with a boat in the center which has an obelisk for a mast (the Tiberine Islet); on this boat are a snake symbolizing the Temple of Esclulapius and an eagle representing the Temple of Jupiter.

Above: a partial view of the Fountain of Rome as it appears today. In the 19th century it was practically all demolished as it was considered dangerous. In the foreground, the boat of the Tiberine Islet, above left, before the statue of Rome, the group of the She-wolf suckling the twins Remus and Romulus, also by Pierre de la Motte. The structure as a whole was undoubtedly conceived by Pirro Ligorio, the Cardinal's archaeologist. - On the lefthand page, below: general view of the Fountain of Rome.

Above: engraving by Venturini (1685) depicting the waterfall of the river Aniene with its rivergod and the Temple of the Sibyl supporting the allegory of the Appennine. - Below: engraving by Venturini (1685): the fountain erroneously called the Hydra Fountain but which actually contained antique statues of Pandora and Minerva, now in the Capitoline Museum.

Grotto of Diana: caryatids in stucco carrying baskets of golden apples; stucco relief depicting Daphne transformed into a tree (above); Perseus and Andromeda; Diana and Callisto (below).

To the left: detail of the ceiling of the Grotto of Diana decorated with stuccos and mosaics. Below: engraving by Venturini (1685) which shows the Fountain of the « Bicchierone » executed by Bernini between 1660 and 1661. - On the righthand page, above: one of the two « metae sudantes » located in the flat section of the garden. These « metae », which are imitations of the famous fountain of ancient Rome rising near the Colosseum and the Arch of Constantine, were originally supposed to have been put up in the middle of the central fishponds. However, they were not executed until the second half of the 17th century when they were set up in the Rotunda of the Cypresses. - Below: rustic fountain with a grotesque mask by the Oval Fountain.

Above: engraving by Venturini (1685) depicting the two metae sudantes set up on the Rotunda of the Cypresses. - Below: engraving by Venturini (1685) showing the Fountain of the d'Este Eagles.

Fountain of the d'Este Eagles.

Diana of Ephesus, copy of antique statue in the Farnese Collection sculpted in travertine by the Flemish artist Gilles van den Vliete. In the documents regarding the villa it is mentioned as the Goddess of Nature or Fortune and was originally placed in the central niche of the Organ fountain which was thus known as the Fountain of the Goddess of Nature. In 1611 the statue was removed and placed at the end of the garden where it is now the main element of a rustic fountain.

TYBVR VVLGO
TIVOLI

THE AQUEDUCTS

One of the problems which arose as soon as the terrain had been properly prepared was that of providing the water required for the fountains.

The accounts ledger reveals that in 1560 a certain Camillo de Martio received payment for the construction of the Rivellese Aqueduct which was to serve the needs of the community of Tivoli, the Franciscan monastery, and the villa. We know that Cardinal Ippolito contributed a third of the expenses out of his own pocket, while the rest was shared by the city government and the prior of the monastery. The cistern for the aqueduct (which carries drinking water) is in Piazza Santa Maria Maggiore. Three storage tanks are located beneath the courtyard of the villa; these provided water for the Pegasus, Rome, and Dragon Fountains, and still supply the main building and the secret garden today.

Nevertheless, when the Organ Fountain and the others were being built, the fountaineers protested that there was hardly enough water and thus a new aqueduct would have to be erected. Zappi narrates: « They ordered that a great quantity of water be transported there by means of a new aqueduct starting from the Oval in the aforesaid garden, eight *palmi* (c. 4 feet) high, five wide, which goes underground through the city of Tivoli and comes out in our river Aniene by the waterfall known as Pelagus and at the mouth of the waters by Monte Catillo a walled structure was put up, having locked doors so that nobody could enter. This aqueduct turned out to be 800 *palmi* long. »

Zappi goes on to report that as soon as the aqueduct was finished he had the opportunity to walk through it lit up by torchlight and that the Cardinal had put up a reward for the man who brought him the news that the job was completed.

Since we have no specific reference concerning the time it took to carry out the project, the dating of the second aqueduct must be placed not before 1563 and not after 1565, as the Cardinal's architect, G. Galvani, who might well have been the project supervisor, informs us.

The arrival of water from the Aniene meant that the fountains became, and are to this very day, the villa's most remarkable feature. The sound of the water, sometimes a murmur and sometimes a roar, permeates the garden and enthralls the beholder who has come to partake of its beauty.

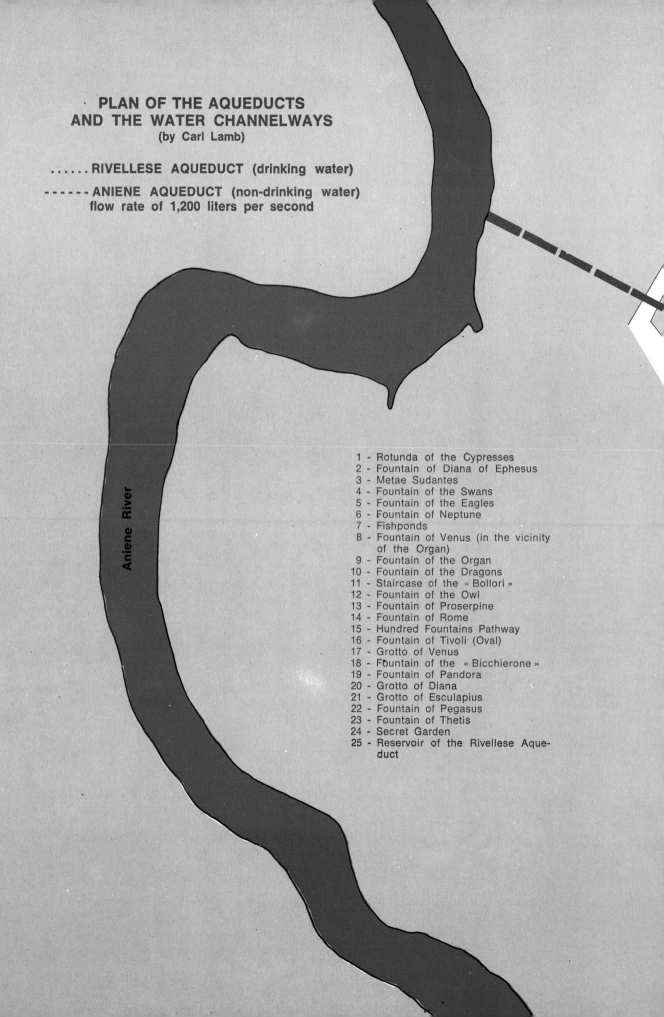

PLAN OF THE AQUEDUCTS
AND THE WATER CHANNELWAYS
(by Carl Lamb)

...... RIVELLESE AQUEDUCT (drinking water)

- - - - - - ANIENE AQUEDUCT (non-drinking water)
flow rate of 1,200 liters per second

Aniene River

1 - Rotunda of the Cypresses
2 - Fountain of Diana of Ephesus
3 - Metae Sudantes
4 - Fountain of the Swans
5 - Fountain of the Eagles
6 - Fountain of Neptune
7 - Fishponds
8 - Fountain of Venus (in the vicinity
    of the Organ)
9 - Fountain of the Organ
10 - Fountain of the Dragons
11 - Staircase of the « Bollori »
12 - Fountain of the Owl
13 - Fountain of Proserpine
14 - Fountain of Rome
15 - Hundred Fountains Pathway
16 - Fountain of Tivoli (Oval)
17 - Grotto of Venus
18 - Fountain of the « Bicchierone »
19 - Fountain of Pandora
20 - Grotto of Diana
21 - Grotto of Esculapius
22 - Fountain of Pegasus
23 - Fountain of Thetis
24 - Secret Garden
25 - Reservoir of the Rivellese Aque-
     duct

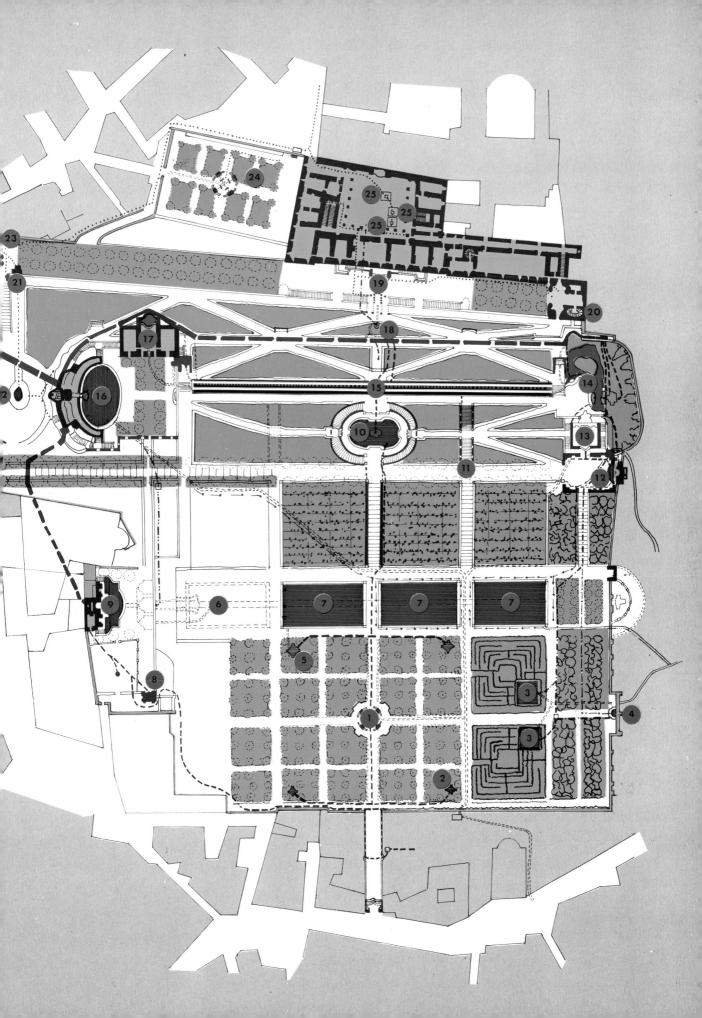

Engraving by Venturini (1685): view of the central zone of the Pathway of the Hundred Fountains. The terracotta high reliefs with scenes taken from Ovid's Metamorphoses are clearly visible.

THE SYMBOLISM OF THE GARDEN

Marc-Antoine Muret ([14]) wrote, « Hard labor never vanquished Hercules, nor sweet pleasure the chaste spirit of chaste Hippolytus. » So, for the sake of both these virtues (strength and chastity), Ippolito (d'Este) dedicated these gardens to Hercules and Hippolytus. The golden apples that Hercules stole from the sleeping dragon in the Garden of the Hesperides now belonged to Hippolytus-Ippolito, who, in remembrance, wanted these gardens to be consecrated to the donor (Hercules) ([15]).

Dedicatio hortorum Tiburtinorum
Aurea sopito rapuit quae mala Dracone
Alcides, eadem nunc tenet Hippolytus.
Qui memor accepti, quos hic conserverat hortos,
Auctori voluit muneris esse sacros.

He died in Rome in 1585.

([14]) Marc-Antoine Muret was born in Muret (Limoges) in 1526. In 1554, accused of immoral acts in Toulouse, he was condemned to be burned at the stake. But he managed to flee to Italy where he became a priest and devoted himself to teaching in various cities. A cultured Humanist, his discourses were highly appreciated for their elegant style and linguistic perfection. He wrote numerous commentaries on classical texts and several works directly in Latin, among which is the *Orationes, epistolae et poemata*. This work contains the two brief poems dedicated to the garden of the Villa d'Este which provided the key to interpreting the symbolism of the villa.

Dedicatio hortorum Tiburtinorum
Nec labor Alciden fregit, nec blanda voluptas
Unquam animum casti molliti Hippolyti.
Ambarum nos hortos virtutum accensus amore,
Herculi et Hippolyto dedicat Hippolytus.

([15]) The eleventh of the Twelve Labors that Eurystheus imposed on the Greek hero Hercules was the conquest of the golden apples given by Gea to Juno on occasion of her wedding to Jupiter. The golden apples were kept in a garden in a land of the Hyperborei (Mauritania) by the Hesperides, i.e. the nymphs of the west, namely Egle, Arethusa, and Hyperthusa, and by the hundred-headed dragon, Ladonis.

Engraving by Venturini (1685): Fountain of Bacchus in a grotto by the Oval Fountain which was originally called the Grotto of Venus and symbolized profane love as opposed to chastity symbolized by the Grotto of Diana. In the central niche of this fountain was a Venus like the Capitoline statue with two little cupids and geese nearby. After the death of Cardinal Ippolito, probably in the time of Cardinal Alessandro, the Venus was replaced by the Bacchus and the two putti and geese were placed on the Fountain of the Swans in the lower section of the garden.

This dedication is the key to the main symbolic scheme of the garden: the Labors of Hercules (related to the efforts of the Cardinal to level the mountain of Tivoli) and that of the golden apples of the Hesperides (which appeared on the coat-of-arms of the House of d'Este) under the protection of the eagle). On the other hand, Hercules was beloved by the whole d'Este family who, imitating the legendary monarchs of Antiquity, had traced their origins back to Hercules and Galatea.

The statues of Hercules were placed along the garden's main axis; a gigantic Hercules holding a club stood in the great niche behind the Fountain of the Dragons, another giant one in the upper grotto depicted him as an old man reclining., while a

third one, showing him with the boy-hero Telephus was placed, in keeping with the axis of the others, in another grotto higher up. The symbolism is centered upon and develops from the Fountain of the Dragons: here is the crossroads that leads to either virtue (Grotto of Diana) or else vice (Grotto of Venus). The triumph of virtue was alluded to by the statues of Achilles and Hercules (immortality and victory over vice) placed on the main staircase.

The Fountain of the Dragons and the niche with the statue of Hercules recall the venture of the hero who managed to steal the golden apples in the Garden of the Hesperides right from under the dragon's nose. The grotto with Venus leaving the bath symbolizes profane love and the fountain with Diana,

Engraving by Venturini (1685): the Fountain of Venus in the vicinity of the Organ Fountain.

together with the virginal Lucretia ([16]), the queen of the Amazons Hippolyte, and Minerva, is a celebration of chastity. But there is also a third symbolism, having to do with geography, not unlike that already encountered in the Audience Hall of the palace.

([16]) According to legend, Lucretia was a Roman matron, the wife of L. Tarquinius Collatinus. The son of Tarquinius the Proud, Sextus Tarquinius, attracted to her great beauty, tried to court her but, rebuffed, he took her by force. Lucretia, overcome with sorrow and shame, committed suicide. Thereupon, the Roman people who were tired of similar abuse revolted against the tyrant Tarquinius, then busily engaged in besieging Areda, and closed the city gates on him so that he would never again be able to enter the city (510 B.C.).

This starts out at the Fountain of Tivoli (Oval) where the three Tiburtine rivers have their origin. We continue along the Path of the Hundred Fountains (the Tiburtine territories) until the three rivers flow into the Fountain of Rome to form the Tiber which in turn was originally supposed to empty into the Fountain of Neptune (representing the sea).

Between 1586 end 1620, since Ippolito's will, modified by his first successor Luigi in exclusive favor of the d'Este family, was still awaiting judgment, the d'Estes, fearing a sentence against them, decided to remove all the statues that could be carried off. In 1621 Alessandro d'Este, once the final changes to the will had been obtained, had all the statues previously removed put back in place.

Engraving by Venturini (1685): the so-called Fountain of the Swans, built in the lower part of the garden shortly after the death of Cardinal Ippolito. The putti and geese which once belonged to the main fountain of the Grotto of Venus are visible.

Beforehand he sponsored a completion and restoration campaign which according to the manuscript preserved in the Modena Archives cost him 26,000 *scudi*. The addition of new fountains such as the Fountain of Venus by the Organ Fountain and the Swan Fountain at the far end of the garden, the replacements and switching around, such as the Jupiter in place of the Hercules and the Bacchus in place of Venus, so greatly altered the thematic links among the sculptures that the original scheme of their symbolic meanings was upset to the point of losing all consistency.

The times, from the death of Ippolito to the advent of his descendant Alessandro, had greatly changed. The authority of the d'Estes was waning in both the political and cultural spheres, while at the same time the Renaissance *Weltanschauung*, based upon Humanistic ideals and re-evocations of the pagan world were being replaced by the Counter-Reformation's much harsher viewpoint, according to which the original concept, so very profane, seemed utterly out of place. Indeed it is likely that the modifications made by Alessandro d'Este, with the resulting loss of the celebrative symbolism that had originally inspired the design of the villa, hardly came about by accident. We can only reconstruct — as best we can through documents — the whole and the details so that we may rediscover the spirit with which it was conceived and only partially brought to life.

PIRRO LIGORIO

Tradition has always credited Pirro Ligorio with the design of the villa and the garden and the latest scholarly works, including Coffin's depth study, do confirm the attribution. Although absolute proof has never turned up, it must also be remembered that such proof is lacking for other firm attributions, some even more famous than the Villa d'Este.

Pirro Ligorio was born into a noble Neapolitan family c. 1513-1514. After receiving a literary-artistic education, he most likely was placed under the tutelage of an established artist so that he could master the arts of painting and drawing. We have no record of who his teachers were, but his style and passion for architecture lead us to believe that they belonged to the Humanistic-artistic circles then flourishing in Naples. From his masters, Ligorio absorbed a knowledge of Latin and « antique culture » which later brought him fame as one of the most knowledgeable scholars of Antiquity in his day. His competence grew and developed in Rome where we find him in 1534, busily engaged in decorating palace façades. One of the earliest works definitely attributed to him is the fresco decoration of the Oratory of San Giovanni Decollato (St. John the Beheaded). The murals portray the Dance of Salome and the Beheading of the Baptist. Although it has been suggested that he worked in the studio of a painter connected with the school of Raphael, it was Michelangelo, whose style then dominated the art world, who had the greatest influence on him in his formative years.

That Ligorio was accepted as member of the « Associazione dei Virtuosi del Pantheon » (the Virtuosi Association of the Pantheon) is proof of his solid reputation as an artist of great intellectual stature. In fact, this society which was founded by Desiderio and Pietro d'Aiutorio in 1542 and headed by Antonio da Sangallo in 1546 served to unite the elite of the art and scholarly worlds of the day.

In 1549 Ligorio entered the service of Cardinal Ippolito who commissioned him to paint one of the friezes of the Monte Giordano palace in Rome. From 1550 to 1554 he served as the Cardinal's personal « antiquario » at the yearly salary of seven scudi and seven baiocchi. This position entailed a complex job: he was in charge of exploring and excavating Hadrian's Villa at Tivoli, after which measurements of the ruins had to be taken. Ligorio drew up three reports on the digs and made a drawing of the villa itself.

We might logically suppose that among the many personages belonging to Cardinal Ippolito's circle it was Ligorio who discussed the plans for the new villa with him. Clearly Ippolito's villa drew its inspiration from Hadrian's Villa. Not only were the architectural and decorative elements influenced, but also the cultural references are related and even the numerous art works then being unearthed had their importance.

The complex of the Hundred Fountains with its reliefs based on Ovid's Metamorphoses reveals more than any other this erudite passion for antiquity. Then too the Oval-Tivoli Fountain (Hadrian's Villa at the time was known as « Old Tivoli »), which architecturally speaking is the most important and original part of the whole undertaking, undoubtedly represents a highly-refined, highly-developed re-elaboration of the Hadrianesque architectural motifs. And this holds true not only for particular structures, as had already been noted (in the comparison of the Oval Fountain to the Canopus of Hadrian's Villa), but even entails a more sweeping connection, i.e. in the overall use of the curvilinear which appeared for the first time in such scale in Hadrian's villa-city.

Nevertheless Hadrian's Villa was not alone in influencing Ligorio while he was working on the new d'Este villa: he had in fact measured and drawn up the plans of the huge hexagonal Villa degli Acilii on the Pincio Hill and the monumental complex of the Sanctuary of Fortuna at Palestrina. The idea for the design probably came to Ligorio from the sanctuary where curvilinear forms were used for the first time in Roman architecture. Due to insurmountable differences in the environmental conditions, Hadrian's Villa could not have provided such a solution whereas the sanctuary bore similarities to the villa being built, in both size and terrain configuration.

In fact, there was an important problem which had to be solved, i.e. unlike the other Renaissance villas located on flat or relatively flat land evened out by terracing, the land destined for the garden of the Villa d'Este lay upon a steep slope. Consequently, since an asymmetrical layout would have marred the unity of the building-garden complex (which had happened in Hadrian's Villa and numerous Renaissance equivalents), the sole solution lay in an axial composition broken up by narrow orthogonal terraces and the use of transversal and oblique ramps to overcome the problem of the uneven terrain. This is exactly what had been done seventeen centuries before in the Sanctuary of Palestrina.

The axial composition, in addition to providing unity to the whole, also provided — just as in the sanctuary — the scenic element, which thus resulted complete whether the viewpoint was the lower en-

Reconstruction of the Temple of Fortuna Primigenia at Palestrina in a drawing by the
architect Furio Fasolo.

trance or the palace overlooking the slope with the
garden below, out towards the plains of Rome.
And of course we are well aware of the important
role played by the scenic in Ligorio's architectural
compositions.

All these factors — a « permanent post » at the
service of the d'Este family, excavation and study of
Hadrian's Villa and the artworks found there, drawings made of the sanctuary and the Roman villas of
Rome and Tivoli, literary background and a passion
for imitating antiquity, constant use of the scenic element — would seem more than enough to confirm the
traditional attribution of the Villa d'Este to Pirro Ligorio, despite the lack of an actual commission
among the partial documents we have on hand.
Perhaps there was no real need for a proper con-
tract. It is more than likely that in times so prone
to pomp and circumstance such a vast celebrative
conception would fit into Ippolito d'Este's grandiose
ambitions. Who else would he have turned to at
such time if not his personal antiquarian-architect?

When work on the villa came to a halt during
the papacy of Paul IV (1555-1559), Ligorio's activity
continued in Rome where he was appointed papal
architect for the new Vatican building projects.
During this period he started work on the Casino
in the Vatican Gardens (which later came to be
known as the Villa Pia or Casino of Pius IV after
the pope in whose reign it was completed). Together
with Rocco° da Montefiascone he covered the walls
of the Casino with stucco reliefs and countless decorative motifs mostly in his typical style stressing the
scenic element. During this period he summarized
his accomplishments as an « antiquario » in forty
voluminous manuscripts on the antiquities of Rome
which he intended to publish and which were anx-

iously awaited by the whole intellectual world. Of
the forty planned, only a slender volume entitled
« Book by Pirro Ligorio Neapolitan Concerning the
Roman Antiquities » ever appeared (actually it was
meant as the preface to the magnum opus). Published
in Venice in 1553, it discusses the circuses, theaters,
and amphitheaters of ancient Rome and reveals the
critical methods Ligorio used in the identification of
Roman monuments. Unfortunately, in order to de-
fend his theories, Ligorio did not hesitate to insert
inscriptions he himself had made up in the antique
style as part of the genuine documentary evidence.
This did much to harm his reputation and cast
suspicion on his whole oeuvre. Then in 1558 he
published another book, this time on the Baths of
Diocletian.

During the following years, he took part in the
projects of the Palazzo della Sapienza and the Belvedere Court in the Vatican. For the latter he designed the curvilinear-shaped covering of the niche.
It too was evidently inspired by the Sanctuary of
Palestrina. At the same time, he was involved in
building the Palazzo Torres, now known as Palazzo
Lancellotti, in Piazza Navona and was also supervisor of the work then being carried out on the
d'Este buildings in Rome, i.e. the Quirinal and
Monte Giordano Palaces, and at Tivoli. He got into
a quarrel with Michelangelo to the point that the
peppery old Florentine threatened to abandon the
St. Peter's project if Ligorio did not stop interfering.
When Michelangelo died, Ligorio was appointed
supervisor of St. Peter's along with — but out-
ranking — Vignola. During these years he gave
vent to his restless, belligerent personality (he liked
to sign himself « Meisopogniro » i.e. « hater of evil
men »). In 1565 he was imprisoned, although the

Engraving by Venturini (1685) showing the façade of the palace.

reason has not come down to us; Ligorio himself blamed his imprisonment on the « intrigues of Della Porta » (he was finally released thanks to the intercession of Cardinal Alessandro Farnese, then sponsor of the Virtuosi of the Pantheon). In 1567 Pope Pius IV removed him from his position as Architect of St. Peter's, perhaps because he wanted to alter Michelangelo's design and, since he had no other official commitments, he returned to his old patron, Cardinal Ippolito, in Tivoli.

Ligorio's name crops up again in the documents as supervisor of the work then being carried out in Tivoli by the artists G. B. Della Porta, G. A. Galvani, and Curzio Maccarone. It was Della Porta who sculpted the sibyls for the Oval Fountain designed by Ligorio and Pierre de la Motte who carved the statue of Rome for the fountain of the same name, also designed by Ligorio. This would explain — though there is no mention of a salary paid out to Ligorio in the ledgers — the frequent gifts that the Cardinal showered upon him, e.g. 23 *scudi* and 30 *baiocchi* in 1567.

Two other artists besides Ligorio also took part in the Villa d'Este project: Gerolamo Muziano (1528-1592) and G. A. Galvani from Ferrara. The latter had previously worked for the Cardinal at the Quirinal Palace in 1563. From the ledgers we learn that Muziano was an interior decoration painter, whereas Galvani was employed as an architect at an annual salary of six *scudi*; he is responsible for the Fountain of the Twisted Columns (Proserpine).

Ligorio must also be credited with an expert knowledge of hydraulic devices which he gained from reading Vitruvius and Hero of Alexandria. « Those who desire to make waterdrawn devices, » he wrote (Turin Manuscript), « have to learn that water power is derived from automatic machines moved by striking wheels, as the devices of Hero and Philostratus. »

At the death of Cardinal Ippolito, the general layout of the villa had already been completed. Pirro Ligorio, sensing that the times had changed, applied for and was granted a permanent post under the patronage of Duke Alfonso II as antiquarian, architect, and artistic advisor. He died in Ferrara in October in the year 1583.

THE ANTIQUE STATUES OF THE VILLA

From Cardinal Ippolito's day onwards, the statues adorning the Villa d'Este were considered one of the major drawing cards and wonders of the whole villa, for both quantity and artistic worth. In these pages, however, we shall not go into a discussion of the numerous statues created by the artists who were contemporaries of the Cardinal. Their sculptures in travertine, peperino, stucco, and terracotta made up (and in many cases still do) a large part of the fountain decoration.

The antique statues are of much greater importance. The documents which have enabled us to draw up an approximate inventory of these treasures are preserved in the State Archives of Modena. Published by Seni, they were amplified by Zappi and later by Del Re. Lastly, Ashby's methodic fruitful research has proved extremely helpful.

Document no. 6 of the Modena Archives contains the inventory reproduced below. Its major interest lies in the quotations given for the pieces.

Greek marble bust depicting Meleager, unsual antique work of excellent workmanship (now in the Capitoline Museum)	1000	scudi
Antique Greek marble statue of a naked Venus (?)	400	»
Two antique, fake marble statues of Amazons of fine and elegant workmanship (now in the Capitoline)	800	»
Another antique Greek marble statue of excellent workmanship and with fine drapery, named Ion (Capitoline)	350	»
Statue of Abundance, with exquisite drapery in dark antique marble and hands in white marble, of excellent workmanship (?)	200	»
Ancient Egyptian basalt statue with dark hair, 10 palmi high, unique piece (Louvre)	2000	»
Exquisite antique statue of a faun in Greek marble of extraordinary workmanship (Capitoline)	400	»
Another antique statue of a faun similar to above, but damaged (?)	250	»
Extraordinary antique statue in Parian marble depicting a Cupid, perfectly executed Greek work	2000	»
Another statue in the same marble, like the one above, but of less perfect workmanship	400	»
Statue of Pallas, 9 palmi high, in Parian marble wearing a paludament with a shield and holding a spear and lorica decorated with the head of the Gorgon, fine antique workmanship (Capitoline)	1000	»
Life-size statue of Diana the huntress shooting an arrow with a dog at her heels, outstanding Greek work (Capitoline)	1000	»
Antique statue, 11 palmi high, of Hercules completely nude with a lion's skin over his head: in his left hand he is supporting his son whose mother was the nymph Augus, near the deer who is nursing the child, while in his right hand he is holding a club; antique piece of fine workmanship, and all carved from a single block (Louvre)	600	»
Antique statue of Pandora, about 10 palmi high, well-draped, showing her carrying the fabulous box of evils with her hand wrapped in her paludament (Capitoline)	200	»
Antique statue of Jupiter seated, holding a thunderbolt, about 10 palmi, of competent workmanship (Ince)	400	»
Antique white marble statue and another life-size statue of a Nymph with butterfly wings; fine, but damaged, work (Capitoline)	150	»
Another statue, like the one above, of a seated Nymph, but even more damaged (?)	60	»
Large-sized antique statue of Mars, about nine palmi high, beautifully carved in white marble (Ince)	200	»
Three other similar antique statues in the same marble depicting pileated freedmen at 80 scudi each (Ince)	240	»
Another marble statue resting upon a tripod wholly carved with bas-reliefs of foliage and grapevine designs with in the center a wholly fluted and ornamented column, and several seahorses depicted upon the basin; antique piece of excellent workmanship	300	»
	11950	scudi

This first inventory gives some idea of the importance and value of the statues then belonging to the villa, but later documents prove that the number of statues was considerably increased after the Cardinal's death, especially during the time of Cardinal Alessandro.

From Del Re's description we learn that the Secret Garden contained a Venus with a cupid astride the dolphin at her feet, a Venus leaving the bath, a statue of Ceres with a torch, a Vestal Virgin,

Engraving by Venturini (1685): the Fountain of Venus, in the room of the villa which led
to the secret garden, with a sleeping Venus. At either side of the basin there were antique
statues.

a Jupiter with an eagle. Four statues standing approximately five *palmi* high were placed upon the railing of the double loggia.

The Modena State Archives also preserves the documents pertaining to the negotiations carried out by the King of Naples with the d'Este family for the purchase of the entire collection. The bargaining was broken off because Cardinal Valenti who represented Pope Benedict XIV made a better offer: 5,000 *scudi* for only fourteen of the statues — which was the price offered by the King of Naples for the whole lot. This group which included the finest works in the collection (e.g. the resting Satyr by Praxiteles, the Cupid, the two Amazons, the Psyche, etc.) was later donated, on May 25, 1753, to the Capitoline Museum by Benedict XIV. Despite the sale of some, many of the valuable pieces were left in the villa. In fact, when Winckelmann was commissioned by Cardinal Alessandro Albani to select pieces for his collection, he recommended a statue of Esculapius, as well as statues of a philosopher, a

rivergod, and a personification of the Nile.

An inventory drawn up by Pannini and Zoboli showed that in about 1768-1769 there were sixty-five statues left. A number of these came into the possession of the Roman merchant Giuseppe d'Este who sold them to the English art dealer Jenkins. They were then bought by Blundell and Smith Barry for the Ince and Marbury collections. The statues mentioned in the Ince collection are: Jupiter, Juno, Mercury, Ancirrus, Cybel, Mars, a cupid with a goose, Julia, hermaphrodite, a head of a rivergod, a wind sarcophagus (not identified), a sarcophagus with hunting scenes. The statue of Zeus enthroned was purchased by the Marbury Collection.

In 1774 there were still seven statues left in the villa. By order of Duke Francesco III they were sent off to Modena to be used to decorate his villa at Sassuolo.

Most of the statues of the Villa d'Este were discovered in Hadrian's Villa, on the Palatine Hill, or elsewhere in and around Rome.

Foto Franco D'Alessio

VICISSITUDES OF THE VILLA D'ESTE

The construction of the villa cost Cardinal Ippolito over 100,000 ducats and a great deal of additional expense was incurred by his successors, especially Cardinal Alessandro d'Este. The citizens of Tivoli were not very enthusiastic about the Cardinal's huge undertaking, and, as a matter of fact, they accused him of wasting tax money and failing to perform his duty towards the community. They complained of the fact that in order to make room for his garden, he had ordered the razing of a hospital that was never rebuilt and that he had paid only token sums for the land he had confiscated. He was also much criticized for having caused great bother to the people living near the villa grounds as he had barred access to their homes from the lower city. A number of local citizens banded together so they could formally charge the Cardinal with these alleged abuses but the matter never went any further and in fact when the Cardinal died, the charges died with him.

For the sake of the record, we must add that Ippolito always was exceedingly generous with the people of Tivoli, for it was clear from his behavior that he had chosen Tivoli as his second homeland. For example, he had the Cathedral rebuilt and commissioned considerable restoration of the church of Santa Maria Maggiore (now San Francesco); he fortified the city and levelled the road leading to it (previously the road was steep and treacherous for man and beast). When in 1564 the Aniene flooded Tivoli with tragic consequences for the local population, he paid for the most urgent repairs out of his own pocket. The sum was later supplemented by a donation of 1900 *scudi* offered by Pope Pius IV then on a visit to Tivoli. He had also strongly supported a motion that the city's wealthiest citizens band together in an association to set up a local wool factory which would have been of great benefit to commerce; for this purpose he had decided to allocate a large sum of money, but the proposal was never taken into serious consideration by those who counted (Beni). He was also a forerunner of modern ecologists. In fact, as Zappi reports, the Cardinal ordered that care be taken of the surrounding mountains in the sense that deforesting (as was then the custom) be strictly forbidden. In governing the difficult community of Tivoli he made full use of the special tact and diplomatic skill he was famous for throughout the major Europeans courts. He always revealed an inborn sense of moderation, without letting himself be intimidated by either man or objects, and all his actions were regulated by his sense of justice (Zappi).

The remarkable beauty and importance of the villa were greatly renowned even during the Cardinal's lifetime. The first to sing its praises was Niccolò Cusano who, as envoy of the Imperial House of Vienna, wrote to the Emperor Maximilian II that the Cardinal from Ferrara had built in Tivoli a royal palace full of statuary and marvelous fountains, the likes of which he had never seen anywhere else in all of Christendom. This letter most likely did much to arouse the Emperor's curiousity, for in 1571 Cardinal Ippolito himself sent a plan of the villa along with several pieces of antique statuary that the emperor had ordered. The plan was drawn up by Étienne Dupérac and it was from this drawing that in 1573 the same artist made the famous engraving he dedicated to Caterina de' Medici, mother of Charles IX of France. This engraving, with slight modifications, was often copied by other artists throughout the 17th century.

Marc-Antoine Muret, the Cardinal's great friend who was also a frequent visitor to the villa in Tivoli, wrote a number of poems to celebrate and describe the beauty of the villa. These poems were extremely helpful in arriving at an interpretatation of the villa's symbolic scheme (Coffin). In addition, Michel de Montaigne who was a guest at the villa in 1581 also helped spread the news of the beauty of the fountains through a report published in his *Journal de Voyage en Italie*.

The major restoration campaigns carried out by Cardinal Alessandro were reported by Antonio Del Re in 1611 (Chapter V of *Dell'Antichità Tiburtine*). In 1685 the engravings which imprinted the public image of the fountains were published by Venturini. Later in 1733 the prints by Piranesi were published. In 1760 Jean Honoré Fragonard lavished all his enthusiasm and admiration, albeit with his usual delicate touch, on a series of sanguines portraying the fountains of the villa (Today these are practically all preserved in the Museum of Besançon).

Many other well-known visitors streamed to Tivoli from all over Europe. The garden and fountains had a widespread and quite determining influence on numerous Italian villas and European gardens. When the villa as a total architectural complex was not utilized as a model, the fountains, especially the Oval Fountain, were taken as models for the fountains of Villa Aldobrandini at Frascati, Villa Lante at Bagnaia, and others in Italy.

According to Pacifici, Luigi Vanvitelli was at Tivoli before designing the Villa Reale at Caserta. In the Villa Reale along the central axis of the garden the four great pools terminate at a waterfall just as in Villa d'Este the fishponds flow into the waterfall of the Organ Fountain.

The names of Tivoli and the Villa d'Este became synonymous with beauty and enjoyment. In fact, many places, even though they have nothing architecturally in common with it, were named after the Villa d'Este, such as the Villa d'Este of Cernobbio and the Tivoli Amusement Park of Copenhagen.

The 18th century witnessed the beginning of the villa's decline. The garden fell into neglect and in 1795 under Ercole III d'Este the sale of the antique statues was completed. Upon the death of Ercole in 1797, the villa was inherited by his daughter Maria Beatrice, wife of Archduke Ferdinand of Austria. Unhappily, in the hands of the Hapsburg Dynasty it fell into total decay. For a short while it came back to life when in 1850-1896 Cardinal Gustav von Hohenlohe commissioned a restoration project. One of the cardinal's guests was Liszt who spent the last years of his life in the villa and, awed by its beauty, composed the exquisite symphony « The Fountains of the Villa d'Este » in praise of it.

In 1918 the Villa d'Este became property of the Italian state. It was restored and opened to the public. Seriously damaged in bombings during World War II, it was once again restored. Finally, in the early sixties, under the supervision of the director of the time, Dr. Roberto Vighi, floodlighting was put in and it thus became one of the most visited sights in the world.

We may conclude by saying that although the Villa d'Este went up at the same time as others such as the Villa Giulia, the Villa Lante of Bagnaia, and the Villa Farnese of Caprarola, it undoubtedly embodied something truly new. Better still, the villa may be defined as the architectural fulfillment of what Bramante (in the Belvedere) and Raphael (in the Palazzo Madama) had forecast years before: a villa based upon a clear and simple architectural composition centered upon a long axis which, from a gateway, leads up to a palace set on high.

This central axis, which serves to align palace and garden as well as to connect flat and irregular terrain, constitutes the most original element of the villa. Even though it was not used for the first time in the Villa d'Este, it was used here more consistently and fruitfully than elsewhere. The major axis is in turn intersected by minor axes creating a clearcut cardus-decumanum (grid) pattern. The broad pathways are broken up by the mirror-like fountains which create pauses for contemplation and at the same time stimulate the spectator to discover the beauty awaiting him at the upper level. In this rhythmic sequence, the pauses are emphasized by the green areas laid out in strictly geometric patterns and this effect is softened by the « water architecture » — be it grandiose, low-key, or elaborate. The whole creates a marvelous scenic view, where the art of man and the art of nature blend together in perfect harmony.

NIGHTTIME SHOWS AT THE VILLA D'ESTE

Nighttime view of the modern Fountain of Neptune (1927)

Fountain of Tivoli (night view).

Nighttime view of the Pathway of the Hundred Fountains.

Fountain of the Owl (night view).

74

Foto Franco D'Alessio

Fountain of the Dragons (night view).

Foto Franco D'Alessio

« Meta sudans » (night view).

CHAPTER INDEX

INDEX OF NAMES, PLACES, AND IMPORTANT MONUMENTS

Detail of the « Banquet of the Gods », painted in the center of the ceiling of the Audience Hall.

BIBLIOGRAPHY

ANTONIO DEL RE, *Antichità Tiburtine.* Rome, 1611.

FRANCESCO IMPARATO, Relazione del Bernini sulle fontane e sulla Villa d'Este a Tivoli, in Archivio Storico dell'arte, 1890.

F. SAVERIO SENI, *La Villa d'Este in Tivoli.* Rome, 1902.

THOMAS ASHBY, « The Villa d'Este at Tivoli and the Collection of Classical Sculpture Which It Contained » in *Archaeologia* LXI (1908) p. 244.

P. DE NOLHAC, « Notes sur Pirro Ligorio », in *Melange « Renier ».* Paris, 1886; pgs. 319-28.

G. LUGLI, *Ville e giardini di Roma antica.* Rome, 1919.

VINCENZO PACIFICI, *Ippolito d'Este, Cardinale di Ferrara.* Tivoli, 1920

GIOVANNI MARIA ZAPPI, *Annali e Memorie di Tivoli.* Tivoli, 1920.

L. DAMI, *Il giardino italiano.* Milan, 1924.

V. PACIFICI, *La Villa d'Este.* Tivoli, 1925.

ARDUINO COLASANTI, *Le fontane d'Italia.* Milan-Rome, 1926.

ARTURO JAHN RUSCONI, *Le ville medicee.* Rome, 1938.

GRIMAL, *Les jardins romains.* Paris, 1943.

PIO PECCHIAI, *Roma nel Cinquecento.* Rome, 1948.

GUSTAVO COCCANARI, *Tivoli.* Tivoli, 1951.

FASOLO-GULLINI, *Il Santuario della Fortuna Primigenia a Palestrina.* Rome, 1953.

A. HAUSER, *A Social History of Art.* Turin, 1955-56.

G. ACHILLE MANSUELLI, *Le ville del mondo romano.* Milan, 1958.

DAVID R. COFFIN, *The Villa d'Este at Tivoli.* Princeton, 1960.

J. BURCKHARDT, *La civiltà del Rinascimento.* Florence, 1961.

G. MASSON, *Giardini d'Italia.* Milan, 1961.

ERNA MANDOWSKY e CHARLES MITCHELL, *Pirro Ligorio's Roman Antiquities.* London, 1963.

CARL LAMB, *Die Villa d'Este in Tivoli.* Munich, 1966.

ISA BELLI BARSALI, *Le ville della campagna romana.* Milan, 1970.

ISA BELLI BARSALI, *Le ville di Roma.* Milan, 1970.

FRANCO D'ALESSIO, *La nuova guida di Tivoli.* Tivoli, 1974.

L. B. DAL MASO - ROBERTO VIGHI, *Lazio Archeologico.* Florence, 1975.

LEONARDO B. DAL MASO, *Roma dei Cesari.* Florence, 1976.

ANTONIO VENDITTI, « Le Ville romane e i loro tesori d'arte », in *Boll. Unione Storia ed Arte,* A. XIX N. 1-4 p. 8. Rome, 1976.

LEONARDO B. DEL MASO, *Roma dei Papi.* Florence, 1977.

PHOTOGRAPHS BY:

Giancarlo Alù, pages: 7; 9; 11; 15; 16; 26; 27; 46 (below).

Franco D'Alessio, pages: 1; 12; 13; 14; 18; 19; 20; 21; 24; 25; 28; 29; 31; 33; 35; 37; 39; 41; 42; 44; 49; 51; 52; 53 (below); 56; 69; 71; 72; 73; 74; 75; 76; 78.

E.P.T. - Rome, pages: 4; 53 (above); 55.

Foto Gioberti - Rome, pages: 22; 27; 30; 32; 34; 36; 38; 40; 42; 46 (above); 48; 50; 52 (below); 54; 60; 61; 62; 63; 66; 68.

SCALA - Florence, pages: 43; 47; 48 (below).